MEET THE
CANDIDATES
2020

KAMALA HARRIS

A VOTER'S GUIDE

Series Edited by
SCOTT DWORKIN

Compiled and Written by Grant Stern

Skyhorse Publishing

Introduction copyright © 2019 by Scott Dworkin
Compiled and written by Grant Stern

Skyhorse Publishing books may be purchased in bulk at special discounts for
sales promotion, corporate gifts, fund-raising, or educational purposes. Special
editions can also be created to specifications. For details, contact the Special
Sales Department, Skyhorse Publishing, 307 West 36th Street, 11th Floor,
New York, NY 10018 or info@skyhorsepublishing.com.

Skyhorse® and Skyhorse Publishing® are registered trademarks of Skyhorse
Publishing, Inc.®, a Delaware corporation.

Visit our website at www.skyhorsepublishing.com.

10 9 8 7 6 5 4 3 2 1

Library of Congress Cataloging-in-Publication Data is available on file.

Cover design by Brian Peterson

ISBN: 978-1-5107-5026-5
Ebook ISBN: 978-1-5107-5034-0

Printed in the United States of America

CONTENTS

INTRODUCTION TO KAMALA HARRIS

BY SERIES EDITOR SCOTT DWORKIN

Right out of the gate, Senator Kamala Harris is one of the strongest candidates running for president in the 2020 Democratic primary. She has assembled an experienced campaign team and has a mix of grassroots and high-dollar donors. Harris already has a national presence both in person and online that is going to be tough for most other candidates to rival.

The senator has a lot of strengths that are built well for her campaign for president. One thing made clear to me by several friends who have worked with Harris is that she is tireless in her efforts. She won't be outworked, and she rarely takes days off. She is absolutely committed to the progressive cause.

Kamala Harris is an inspirational figure to many. She has been at the forefront of the national progressive movement for the last eight years, ever since being elected as attorney general in the state of California in 2011. When she won her race for the U.S. Senate in 2016, she immediately became one of the leading progressive voices in the chamber.

She reminds me a lot of President Barack Obama. She too has strength and poise, mixed with a brilliant understanding of complex issues and laws and an ability to cut through gibberish and nonsense to get to the core of a matter. She also has fierce negotiating skills and a capacity to present complex issues in an understandable way for the average American. The senator was an early supporter of Obama herself, and she has drawn comparisons to him in the media throughout her political career.

Kamala Harris wants to stand up for folks who can't stand up for themselves, to serve as a voice of hope and reason in a world filled with lies and despair, especially on the campaign trail. And she is promising to weed out all of the rampant corruption that has been ongoing for years in Washington but spread like a wildfire following President Trump's swearing in. She might be the perfect candidate to not only beat Trump but also clean up the mess he's made while in the Oval Office.

The Harris campaign is running on a strong Democratic values platform that incorporates most of the issues you would hope to hear from a progressive candidate—all while being able to keep a serious tone mixed with the uplifting message that Speaker Pelosi crafted for the 2018 midterm election: "For The People."

One of the most prominent issues in Senator Harris's platform is a focus on rebuilding the middle class. She has already pledged on the campaign trail to give the "largest middle class tax cut in a generation."[1]

Another strong part of the Harris campaign platform is her willingness to be a voice in the civil rights movement. One issue that commonly arises is the fact Harris hasn't consistently taken the progressive position on every item in the past, or fought every opponent tooth and nail. But what people might have to realize is that being an attorney general requires you to choose your battles and be willing to negotiate.

Kamala Harris has a strong record of fighting to protect women's rights throughout the country. She's fought for years for reproductive health rights and helped lead the fight for equal pay for women, and she has also led the charge in going to bat for women in film.[2] She has a long track record of supporting progressive values in support of women. The key moment in Senator Harris's national political career was her questioning of Judge Brett Kavanaugh during his Supreme Court confirmation hearings. She flipped the script on the partisan judge and asked Kavanaugh to name a single law governing a man's body. It left Kavanaugh speechless.[3]

When it comes to President Trump and his cronies paying for the crimes they committed, there may be no person better suited to making sure the current administration is held accountable for their corrupt acts than Kamala Harris, who was a career prosecutor for twenty-five years before getting elected to the Senate. She also serves on the Senate Intelligence Committee and has spent time personally on the investigation into Putin's election attack and the failure of social media platforms to protect our democracy.

Harris seems like the kind of prosecutor-in-chief America needs to drain the expanded Trump swamp in DC following the April 18, 2019, release of the Mueller Report. The report revealed that Donald Trump and his team expected help from Russia,[4] and detailed numerous instances in which Trump tried to obstruct justice.[5] In a CNN town hall shortly after the report came out, Senator Harris made it clear that Congress has to follow the facts where they lead, even if that means impeachment.

Harris would be the perfect kind of person to dig in, follow the facts, and deliver justice for the American people.

In the past, the junior senator from California has been criticized for not responding hard enough to big banks and those on Wall Street. Now, one of her talking points on the campaign trail has been how she took on the big banks and will try to clean up Wall Street's mess from the White House. Harris said this in her announcement speech on January 21, 2019:

> And I'll tell you, sitting across the table from the big banks, I witnessed the arrogance of power. Wealthy bankers accusing innocent homeowners of fault, as if Wall Street's mess was of the people's making.[6]

She did win a massive $18 billion settlement for California homeowners from three large banks after the peak of the 2008 financial crisis as a state attorney general. But her follow-up initiatives fell flat.

Harris personally reached out to multiple Wall Street executives for potential support before announcing her run, and even though she pledged to take on Wall Street, she has accepted $798,677 from the securities and investment industry.[7, 8] Her ties to big banks are bound to become a campaign issue at some point. A CNBC article explains one reason why:

> In 2012, the California Department of Justice found in an investigation that OneWest Bank participated in "widespread misconduct" when foreclosing on homes, recommending that Harris file a civil enforcement action against the bank. However, Harris declined to prosecute OneWest or its then-CEO, Steven Mnuchin, despite the

department's recommendation. A spokesman for Mnuchin called the allegations "garbage."

The OneWest issue was resurfaced in 2017 when Mnuchin was nominated to serve as Treasury secretary. She was also the only Democratic Senate candidate to receive a donation from Mnuchin during the 2016 elections, according to FEC records.

So not only did Harris decline to prosecute Trump's Treasury Secretary Steven Mnuchin, her campaign even took a contribution from him in 2016.

Even though Harris asks for and takes money from some corporate leaders, she still has broadly attacked those same people, if only in her public statements and not yet in action. In March of 2018, Harris issued a statement announcing her opposition to a bill aimed to deregulate banks. In it, Harris made her position against Wall Street abundantly clear:

The American people deserve an economy where Main Street is protected from the excesses of Wall Street. After 2008, when Wall Street recklessly triggered the worst financial crisis since the Great Depression, Congress put in place a number of common-sense safeguards to protect taxpayers and reduce the risk of another major recession. The bill that the Senate passed today needlessly weakens those protections.

By shielding nearly two-thirds of the largest banks from tough oversight, reducing transparency, and allowing banks to make mortgages to unqualified buyers, this *bill invites financial institutions to engage in the same risky behavior that led to the Great Recession and cost taxpayers more than $600 billion to bail out the banks.*

This legislation is short-sighted and irresponsible. It's a bonus for the wealthy and powerful—not the American people.

As Attorney General of California, I fought tooth and nail for Californians hit hard by the state and national mortgage crisis, including winning a $20 billion settlement for California homeowners from the big banks. We established a multidivisional Mortgage Fraud Strike Force and passed the 'Homeowners Bill of Rights,' establishing the nation's most comprehensive anti-foreclosure protections. Taxpayers deserve more of these protections, not less.

Congress should not incentivize banks to engage in further reckless behavior and leave American taxpayers to pick up the tab. One financial crisis in the past decade is enough.[9]

Consumer advocacy is a big part of what she represents as a candidate. If there's one thing Americans could expect with a President Kamala Harris, it is that she would fiercely take on bad corporate behaviors, especially those that injure Americans. Part of keeping Americans safe involves making sure companies don't defraud its customers, whether it be with faulty products or outright fraud.

In addition, Senator Harris has pledged to not accept corporate PAC contributions during this campaign. But when candidates make that pledge, it's important to note that most corporations probably wouldn't get involved in a Democratic primary anyway. It would be easy for them to say they wouldn't take sides in order to avoid making a contribution to any candidate. It's like if I said I was not going to go to the Academy Awards next year, even though I wasn't invited. So there isn't really much risk in making a pledge. Large donors provide most of her funds.

Harris has the unique experience as a prosecutor to be able to figure out a way to ensure laws are made without loopholes for corporations. A good example is when then–California Attorney General Harris publicly urged the Consumer Financial Protection Bureau (CFPB) to "adopt consumer protections against harmful practices by payday lenders." She wrote a scathing letter about the payday lending industry to the CFPB, saying:

> *Californians who need short-term emergency access to cash are getting stuck in a destructive and unaffordable cycle of repeat high-interest loans that they cannot afford to repay. Together with California's existing lending laws, the Bureau's proposals would bring needed protections to vulnerable California consumers who take out small-dollar loans, which too often are predatory and create a debt trap for fixed- and low-income borrowers.*[10]

Senator Harris explained her position further in this November 2017 tweetstorm:

The Consumer Financial Protection Bureau is a watchdog agency with the core mission to defend American consumers from predatory and fraudulent practices that can financially ruin you and your family. When I was CA's Attorney General, we had to fight tooth and nail to get relief for struggling families who were put in impossible financial positions by the foreclosure crisis, predatory for-profit colleges, payday lenders, the list goes on.

If we want to fight predatory behavior in the future, we need to maintain a strong @CFPB. Mick Mulvaney, the man Trump is sending in to lead the @CFPB, has called it a "joke." He's flat-out wrong. The American people deserve someone who will stand up and fight for consumers.[11]

If American consumers want a fierce advocate in the White House, then Kamala Harris would be a good choice. This necessity will become more apparent as the campaign goes on, especially given the current White House's moves to try and deregulate every industry as much as possible.[12]

The fund-raising prowess of Harris seems to be limitless. Whether it's her relationships in California with donors at both the state and federal level, or her ability to appeal to some of the wealthiest Democratic donors in the country, Harris will have the ability to fund her campaign at least until Super Tuesday on March 3, 2020.

Keep in mind that California's primary is now included in Super Tuesday. Although delegates are doled out on a proportional basis and it's not a winner-take-all scenario, it's still a crucial moment with a large delegate haul at stake. Harris is the favorite there, but plenty of people have lost their home state in the past when running for president, including Marco Rubio and Jeb Bush, who lost Florida to Trump. Those people usually don't become their party's nominee.

Nevertheless, there are a few issues that Democratic primary voters won't like that the Harris campaign will have to navigate.

The largest issue for the Harris campaign is finding a way to separate herself from the pack in order to pull ahead. The debates will be crucial. If she's able to show America her no-nonsense prosecutorial style of debating while displaying the level of care she has for our country, it might be refreshing for voters to hear. But with so many other candidates, it will be hard for anyone to really move in front swiftly.

Another big issue the campaign will have to face is the fact that Senator Harris owns a gun. Some issues are deal breakers for a lot of Democrats, and this is one of them. There are many Democratic voters who don't support gun ownership in general. Only 25 percent of Democrats have a gun owned by someone in their household, while 57 percent of Republicans have someone in their home who owns a gun.[13] The mere ownership of a gun in this climate might make voters wary of supporting Harris. But at least Harris doesn't hide it; she makes it clear she owns a gun, and has no regrets about it. On April 11, 2019, Harris defended her ownership of a firearm by saying:

> *I am a gun owner, and I own a gun for probably the reason a lot of people do—for personal safety. I was a career prosecutor. We are being offered a false choice. You're either in*

favor of the Second Amendment or you want to take every-one's guns away. It's a false choice that is born out of a lack of courage from leaders who must recognize and agree that there are some practical solutions to what is a clear problem in our country. Part of the practical solution is to agree that we need smart gun safety laws. Period.[14]

In general, though, Kamala Harris's strong stance on gun reform now will definitely still benefit her campaign. She has called for an assault weapons ban and for commonsense gun law reforms across the board, including tighter background checks and eliminating the gun show loophole.[15] No matter what, though, in the Democratic primary you will see her possession of a gun get mentioned by her opponents, especially during the debates. A skilled debater, expect Senator Harris to use the moment when she gets criticized over it to remind people that she was the top law enforcement officer in the state of California, so owning a firearm should not seem that unusual. Still, there will be some people who will never support Harris due to that one fact.

Another complication surrounding the Harris campaign is the involvement of her family members on the campaign. Following the trauma our country has gone through with unqualified family members being in the White House, people might be more cautious than usual with anyone who has family members as senior members of the campaign team. Maya Harris, the senator's sister who serves as the campaign chair, is overwhelmingly qualified for a White House position.[16]

Still, the American people might not like even the potential of having more family members of the president serve as White House staff. We've seen what kind of damage nepotism can do to the country throughout Trump's entire presidency, though the Harris family is 180 degrees opposite of the Trump family in terms of both being extremely hardworking and highly qualified by any objective standard.

Another issue is that other candidates are garnering support from some of the Harris campaign's largest donors, which is natural with so many other prominent candidates joining the race. It's common for donors to throw multiple fund-raisers for different presidential candidates. But it's still troublesome, with split allegiances to multiple candidates, as it leads to less money and support for Harris. Recently, the Pete Buttigieg campaign held multiple fund-raising events in California involving some of Harris's biggest supporters.[17] One large Democratic donor in California that I spoke with in April 2019 said: "I don't care if it's Kamala-Pete, or Pete-Kamala, I think that's the winning ticket."

An additional roadblock to the presidency for Harris is what some might deem to be a questionable campaign donor history.

In addition to soliciting donations from Wall Street, Harris has received a lot of support from donors in Silicon Valley, which makes sense since she's from California, and from big law firms, which also makes sense since she's a lawyer. But that doesn't mean she won't receive intense criticism for it. Since 2015, she's received over $2.3 million from lawyers and law firms alone for her Senate campaign account.[18] Harris took in $128,175 from employees of WarnerMedia Group, $109,776 from Alphabet, Inc., (Google's parent company), $91,273 from employees of the corporate law firm Venable LLP, and $90,402 from employees of 21st Century Fox.[19]

Donations from executives at those companies could be used by candidates like Warren and Sanders to attack Harris—especially via Warren, who is running in the same progressive lane as Harris but has pledged to hold no high-dollar fund-raisers for her campaign.

Harris's largest donations based on employer came from the University of California system, totaling $128,804 since 2015. That's not something others can really attack her for, as professors represent a large donor base for all progressives.

There are a number of challenges that Harris must overcome in her road to the 2020 Democratic primary victory, let alone the White House, but it seems like she's up for the challenge.

To win the primary, her chances will hinge mainly on a combination of outright winning some of the debates and receiving unexpected endorsements, like she has already from members of Congress. She will also have to surpass others in their fund-raising haul. Harris already has started to receive key endorsements from 75 percent of the California state Senate caucus, three U.S. Representatives, and even some key Democrats in South Carolina.[20, 21]

But it's going to be a steep hill to climb.

Both former Vice President Biden and Senator Bernie Sanders have the benefit of having run for president before. They have a larger groundswell of support nationally and better name recognition as well. Harris will have to find a way to overcome the momentum of Sanders and his rabid fanbase, lingering good feelings from the Obama years for Biden, Senator Warren's outstanding policy ideas, and the rising star of Buttigieg, the mayor of South Bend, Indiana. It's doable, but it's going to be a tough road.

If Harris makes it past the primary, she can absolutely beat Donald Trump in a general election, without a doubt in my mind.

Kamala Harris's no-nonsense attitude combined with her tireless work ethic would put Trump to shame. Her commanding presence is presidential, and if she can convey to the American people her sense of urgency about changing the direction of this country, then she might just make it to the Oval Office.

America would be lucky to have Senator Harris in the White House.

WHO IS KAMALA HARRIS?

The defining feature of Senator Kamala Harris is that she's a progressive woman who is determined to make changes for the better and ready to work tirelessly to make it happen. She began a career as an assistant district attorney hoping to learn how to change the system from the inside, and has matured into a leading Democratic senator who doesn't hold back her strong political positions but delivers them with alternating gusto and poise. Harris is a trailblazing figure in her field as a woman and as an African American and a South Asian American who has never lost an election, breaking through glass ceilings in law enforcement.

Her 2020 Democratic candidacy for the presidential primary has attracted a ten-figure fund-raising haul in the early going, and she has spoken to vast crowds early in the campaign. Senator Kamala Harris's key national moment was a pair of senate committee hearings where she used her prosecutorial skills to cross-examine high-ranking members of the Trump administration, especially former Attorney General Jeff Sessions, and her determined drilling of Judge Brett Kavanaugh upon his nomination for the Supreme Court. The Kavanaugh hearings that propelled Harris from a top senator into a true household name among the politically aware people who tend to vote in primary elections and caucuses.

It is fair to say that Senator Harris's campaign is shaped by her professional career in public service, her rhetorical flourishes, and a consistently progressive outlook. Unlike Sanders, Harris isn't an explicitly ideological candidate. Unlike Warren, she's not pushing a specific agenda, though she too does have binders full of bills that she has authored and/or passed in just a short period of time. If there's one strength that Harris displays above all others, it is the ability to connect with her audience and demonstrate a unique combination of empathy as a communicator and strength as a career law enforcement officer. If there's a major weakness in her campaign it is that she has no announced foreign policy—though this might not matter and can be corrected later—and she may struggle to woo some primary voters over when they find out about her mistakes as a prosecutor. "I don't agree with every decision she's made on criminal justice, but then I also know she was a prosecutor," says SiriusXM Progress 127 morning host Mark Thompson, who has personally interviewed Harris multiple times. "So my expectation is that a prosecutor is gonna, a lot of times, make the decisions that an average prosecutor would make."[1]

The Harris campaign hasn't released detailed policy guides in the early stages of the primary race, but the senator has a significant batch of detailed policy in the legislation that she has proposed or prominently cosponsored with some of her opponents in the 2020 primary. Kamala Harris is proposing a tremendous tax cut for America's middle-class earners. She wants to implement a schoolteachers' pay hike that one economist says will pay for itself with cash to spare. Senator Harris is in favor of the Sanders Medicare for All plan, which she has supported for two years now, including eliminating private insurance companies' role in universal coverage, limiting them to the kinds of popular supplemental plans sold in every other indus-trialized nation that treats health care as a human right. Harris's program to help renters who've been suffering from high prices and a supply short-age has its critics, but would go a long way to bringing equity in the tax code to non-homeowners. Her efforts at bipartisan bail reform are worth implementing to help over six hundred thousand Americans who can't afford cash bail and must sit in jail while awaiting trial. Her immigration policies define the progressive viewpoint in that space and her support for the Green New Deal, which she applauds for sparking climate change dis-cussions, places her firmly in the mainstream of the Democratic Party.

As a career prosecutor, Kamala Harris interpreted her role in public life as seeking proactive solutions to problems as she steadily rose through the ranks of county government in Oakland and San Francisco. At the age of thirty-eight, she handily defeated San Francisco's incumbent DA. It was a life-changing moment for Harris. It was a confirmation of the promise that she surely harbored growing up in the Bay Area and later in Montreal, that she could do big things like her immigrant parents, who researched cancer and advised governments on economics. At the same time, her sister Maya Harris followed a parallel track as a civil rights advocate and lawyer, eventually transitioning to politics and now running the campaign for her sister, the senator.

Harris implemented her vision of progressive change in the San Francisco DA's office and at the same time grew her national political pro-file there, culminating in a book, *Smart on Crime: A Career Prosecutor's Plan to Make Us Safer,* and she introduced her first major program, an anti-truancy initiative. That's when she started getting very active in state politics in nearby Sacramento and got her anti-truancy program taken statewide. Simultaneously, she kicked off what would become her first campaign for the statewide office of attorney general. It wasn't an easy race, as an evidentiary scandal rocked the San Francisco district attorney's office that year, but she still won her third election (and only second with an opponent) in a crowded field of Democrats, then later by a razor-thin margin against a Republican opponent from Los Angeles, a larger metropolitan area.

California Attorney General Harris was very active in the legislative process that led to a homeowners' bill of rights and created a department to correct institutional injustices being perpetrated against children. Harris used superlative litigation tactics to win billions of dollars from America's biggest banks for her state's beleaguered mortgage borrowers. However, it was a controversial term of office for her; it included issues with the statewide implementation of one of her top legislative wins, and her office's poor track record on holding local district attorneys accountable when they committed prosecutorial misconduct.

California voters approved her decisions, because she won her fourth term of public office in 2014 with a majority of the votes in both the primary—which is a nonpartisan open race called a "jungle primary"— and by fifteen points in the general election. Two years after that, Harris won a landslide victory in the race for the Senate, which she used to become a top-tier candidate for the 2020 Democratic primary nomination.

Senator Harris did something that is not only unusual for a woman, but something that freshman senators generally just do not do. She forcefully charged into a position of de facto leadership in her caucus, blowing off incidents where her male counterparts tried to shut her down, but without causing the kinds of sexist backlashes that afflicted her predecessors like Hillary Clinton. In just a short tenure in the Senate, Kamala Harris has pulled off a string of victories while serving as one of the minority's most outspoken opponents of the president, whose party is in the majority. Just google "Kamala Harris grilling" and a list of public officials misusing their offices—some with presidential direction—turns up, showing how she used prime committee assignments to move public policy. She has passed several consequential bills, including those for disaster relief and more funding for historically black colleges and universities, and has advanced an anti-lynching bill, which passed the Senate twice and has a good chance of becoming law during the campaign.

Senator Harris's charisma is key to this campaign, and she deftly wields the political ability to flip an issue on its head or divert an attack and turn it into a plus. Her counterattacks can be devastating. In a head-to-head matchup against Donald Trump, she will have to use a different strategy than Hillary Clinton deployed, which focused on his negatives.

Early polling is mixed but shows that Harris can beat President Trump. She is running in third to fifth place across virtually every early poll in the 2020 Democratic primary. Senator Harris raised $12 million in her first quarter with sixty-four days in the race. Her endorsements in the early primary state of South Carolina are piling up, and Harris has already swept the upper echelon of endorsements from California's popular Democratic statewide officials. She must win both states by Super Tuesday to propel her campaign into a condensed schedule of contests in March and early April.

Kamala Harris has her eyes on some of the key Democratic primary voting blocs, and a lot of what she has released is laser focused on serving that base. Women, and particularly women of color, are Harris's base voters. Targeting teachers and renters with new policies is another key area for her campaign, and the senator's legislative proposals are a direct appeal to those voters.

Harris voters know what they'd get with the California senator if elected: a hard-charging advocate for data-driven policies and new ideas to fix income inequality and the justice system, plus an advocate for expanding America's social safety net to improve quality of life across the country.

Notwithstanding her lack of familiarity to most voters, Harris is ready to face the scrutiny of being an early member of the top-tier candidates in 2020. She has already released her taxes for many years. Kamala Harris has been preparing for this campaign for years now, in a way, since the start of her political career when the media and many people who had met her compared her with her peer, former president Barack Obama. "A lot of times when people are given those types of monikers, it's almost a jinx, and they rarely live up to them," says the radio host Thompson. "But, I think in many ways she has done that." The 2020 primary will be the ultimate test of that long-running comparison of Harris to the popular Obama.

There is no question that Senator Harris can maintain a campaign throughout the 2020 Democratic primary. There is also no question that today, her policy plans are attractive to the progressive wing of the Democratic Party. The big question is if Kamala Harris can use the debates to turn her early position up to the point that she can win a solid plurality or majority of the primary votes and capture the Democratic presidential nomination with mainstream approval at the party's national convention.

DEFINING MOMENTS IN HARRIS'S POLITICAL CAREER

S enator Kamala Harris's defining political moments have come early in her first term in Congress and showcased her prosecutorial skills during high-stakes questioning of high-profile Trump appointees in committee hearings. The senator from California displayed her talent for evenhandedly asking the toughest questions of some of the most difficult witnesses—both lawyers—and leaving both men openly begging for mercy or speechless.

Senator Harris's first big splash came when she cornered Attorney General Jeff Sessions with a series of sharp queries in a Senate Intelligence Committee hearing in July 2017.

But it was her patient grilling of Supreme Court nominee Brett Kavanaugh on issues from abortion to his contacts with Donald Trump's law firm that turned her into an overnight political sensation. And that was before she adroitly addressed Professor Christine Blasey Ford's allegations of sexual assault and delivered a fiery speech against Kavanaugh's nomination.

Her piercing interrogations of Judge Brett Kavanaugh happened during the height of the midterm election campaign in the months of September and October 2018, and it translated directly into a favorable early impression among Iowa voters who will participate in the first caucuses of the 2020 Democratic primary.

Six months into Senator Harris's term, her first high-profile moment on the dais arrived in July 2017 when she needled Attorney General Jeff Sessions about his ties to Russian officials during the 2016 presidential campaign, which included numerous contacts with Russia's Ambassador.[1] She lobbed pointed questions at Sessions after he had denied those same ties during his confirmation hearings earlier that year, then abruptly recused himself from the investigation into Russian election interference two months later. Senator Harris was a persistent and outspoken critic of Sessions, tweeting that his nomination to the attorney general position was "troubling" soon after it was announced, sending out over three dozen messages demanding his recusal from the Russian election interference probe, and even calling for his resignation for being involved.[2]

It's rare that a sitting attorney general looks like he wants to literally bolt from the hearing room to avoid answering questions, but Senator Harris's line of questions totally unnerved Sessions. The Mueller Report later revealed that Sessions was then the subject of an active FBI investigation on suspicion of perjury to Congress. The news-making exchange went down after the senator methodically asked a series of questions to narrow down the possible answers for the evasive Alabama politician turned cabinet official:

> SENATORS HARRIS: Did you have any communications with Russian officials for any reason during the campaign that have not been disclosed in public or to this committee?

ATTORNEY GENERAL SESSIONS: I don't recall it but I have to tell you I cannot testify to what was said as we were standing at the Republican convention and before the podium where I spoke. I should—not only don't have a detailed memory of that, ok and I'm going to your knowledge . . .

HARRIS: Did you have any communication with any Russian businessmen or any Russian nationals?

SESSIONS: I don't believe I had any conversation with Russian businessmen or Russian nationals. Are you aware lot of people were at the convention? It's conceivable somebody there, I haven't missed a few, let me qualify it, I if you don't qualify it you'll accuse me of lying, so I need to be correct as best I can. I want you to be I'm not able to be rushed this fast, it makes me nervous.[3]

"It was a simple question," Harris explained later on Twitter.[4] "Can Sessions point to the policy, in writing, that allows him to not answer a whole host of our questions today?"

Social media lit up after the exchange, which ended with the late Senator John McCain (R-AZ) stepping in to shield his former colleague from further questions that he could not or would not answer for which he was making a shamelessly empty excuse.[5] "There goes McCain (who isn't on this committee) interrupting Kamala Harris again," wrote MSNBC anchor Joy Reid, "and admonishing her to be nice."[6] *HuffPost* reporter

Jennifer Bendery asked, "Is it a requirement that Senate Republican men interrupt Kamala Harris *every* time she grills an official giving testimony?"[7] Her newfound fans on social media began taking note, and even mentioning her as a presumptive 2020 presidential nominee.[8]

However, that would only be a small fraction of the response Senator Harris drew from her powerful probing of DC Circuit Court judge Brett Kavanaugh's nomination for the Supreme Court. Again and again, she patiently prodded and then pounced upon Kavanaugh's evasive answers, making him—literally one of the world's few experts in judicial nominations—look out of place at the most controversial Supreme Court nomination hearings of our generation.

It all began right after Labor Day 2018, when Senator Harris got a tip that Judge Kavanaugh had met with a lawyer who worked at the law firm founded by President Trump's longtime attorney. The first two minutes of Harris's questions drilled right in on a key point many Americans wanted to know about the Supreme Court nominee—who Trump surprisingly added to his list of judicial choices *after* getting elected—who is presiding over issues related to the Special Counsel investigation of Russian election interference and the Trump campaign.[9]

> HARRIS: Judge, have you ever discussed Special Counsel Mueller or his investigation with anyone?
>
> KAVANAUGH: Well, it's in the news every day. I . . .
>
> HARRIS: Have you discussed it with anyone?
>
> KAVANAUGH: With other judges I know.

HARRIS: Have you discussed Mueller or his investigation with anyone at Kasowitz, Benson, and Torres, the law firm founded by Marc Kasowitz, President Trump's personal lawyer? Be sure about your answer, sir.

KAVANAUGH: Well, I'm not remembering, but if you have something that you want to . . .

HARRIS: Are you certain you've not had a conversation . . .

KAVANAUGH: I said . . .

HARRIS: . . . with anyone at that law firm?

KAVANAUGH: Kasowitz, Benson . . .

HARRIS: Kasowitz, Benson, and Torres, which is the law firm founded by Marc Kasowitz, who is President Trump's personal lawyer. Have you had any conversation about Robert Mueller or his investigation with anyone at that firm? Yes or no?

KAVANAUGH: Well, is there a person you're talking about?

HARRIS: I'm asking you a very direct question. Yes or no?

KAVANAUGH: I need to know the—I'm not sure I know everyone who works at that law firm.

HARRIS: But I don't think you need to. I think you need to know who you talked with. Who did you talk to?

KAVANAUGH: I don't think I—I'm not remembering, but I'll—I'm happy to be refreshed or if you want to tell me who you're thinking of who works there.

HARRIS: So are you—are you saying that with all that you remember—you have an impeccable memory. You've been speaking for almost eight hours, I think more, with this committee about all sorts of things you remember. How can you not remember whether or not you had a conversation about Robert Mueller or his investigation with anyone at that law firm? This investigation has only been going on for so long, sir, so please answer the question.

KAVANAUGH: Right, I'm not sure I—do I—I'm just trying to think, do I know anyone who works at that firm? I might know . . .

HARRIS: Have you had—that's not my question. My question is, have you had a conversation with anyone at that firm about that investigation? It's a really specific question.

KAVANAUGH: I would like to know the person you're thinking of, because what if there's . . .

HARRIS: I think you're thinking of someone and you don't want to tell us.

[Incredibly awkward pause, while Kavanaugh looks flustered]

Who did you have a conversation with at . . .

KAVANAUGH: I am—I'm not going to . . . [10]

At that moment, Senator Mike Lee (R-UT) jumped in to "save" Kavanaugh from having to answer the question on the spot. Protesters began yelling and were removed from the chamber. Lee had no right to object under the hearing's rules, and Senator Harris was allowed to resume her questioning. After two more minutes of interrogating, the exchange ominously ended:

> *HARRIS: That's fine. I'll ask a more direct question, if that's helpful to you. Did you speak with anyone at that law firm about Bob Mueller's investigation?*
>
> *KAVANAUGH: I'm not remembering anything like that, but I want to know a roster of people and I want to know more.*
>
> *HARRIS: So you're not denying that you've spoken with . . .*
>
> *KAVANAUGH: Well, I said I don't remember anything like that.*
>
> *HARRIS: OK. I'll move on. Clearly you're not going to answer the question.* [11]

The stakes of Senator Harris's questions were high. If Kavanaugh went on the record revealing his discussions about Mueller with any lawyers at the firm who represented Trump for decades in large cases, like the Trump University fraud and racketeering lawsuit, it meant that there would be an appearance of impropriety. If confirmed, then Kavanaugh could be forced by his peers to recuse himself from any decisions about it that go to the Supreme Court. She wasn't finished.

Harris changed tacks again and began asking Kavanaugh questions about race relations in America and the Voting Rights Act, as well as his opinion—which he refused to offer—about the terrible events in Charlottesville which had happened a month prior to the hearing, when a massive gang of white supremacists marched on the Virginia college down, and one murdered an anti-racist protester, Heather Heyer.

Harris then turned to questions about case law that his conservative predecessors Justice Samuel Alito and Chief Justice John Roberts had answered during their confirmations regarding the foundational cases for the right to privacy. Kavanaugh answered the question.

It was a setup.

That's when the California senator pivoted to asking about a woman's right to choose when to reproduce. The conservative judge worked very hard to avoid the question, citing judicial independence. Nevertheless, Senator Harris's questioning left him speechless at times—again—and proved that he didn't want to answer her well-formed questions because the results would at the minimum embarrass him, and, at the worst, a bad answer could have sunk his nomination:

> *HARRIS: Do you believe the right to privacy protects a woman's choice to terminate a pregnancy?*
>
> *KAVANAUGH: That is a question that, of course, implicates Roe v. Wade. And following the lead of the nominees*

for the Supreme Court, all eight current—sitting justices of the Supreme Court have recognized that two principles that are important. One, we shouldn't talk about in this position cases or issues that are likely to come before the Supreme Court or could come before the Supreme Court. And secondly, I think Justice Kagan provided the best articulation of commenting on precedent. She said we shouldn't give a thumbs up or thumbs down.

HARRIS: I appreciate that. And I did hear you make reference to that, that perspective earlier. But you also, I'm sure, know that Justice Ginsburg at her confirmation hearing said, quote, this is—on this topic of Roe—quote, "This is something central to a woman's life, to her dignity. It's a decision she must make for herself. And when government controls that decision for her, she's being treated as less than a fully adult human responsible for her own choices." Do you agree with the statement that Justice Ginsburg made?

KAVANAUGH: So Justice Ginsburg, I think there was talking about something she had previously written about Roe v. Wade. The other seven justices currently on the Supreme Court have been asked about that and have respectfully declined to answer about that or many other preferences, all the—whether it was Justice Marshall about Miranda or about Heller or Citizens United.

HARRIS: And we discussed it earlier.

KAVANAUGH: And it's rooted—I just want to underscore, it's rooted in judicial independence.

HARRIS: No, I appreciate that. But on—but I'm glad you mentioned that Justice Ginsburg had written about it before, because you also have written about Roe when you praised Justice Rehnquist's Roe dissent. So in that way, you and Justice Ginsburg are actually quite similar, that you both have previously written about Roe.

So my question is, do you agree with her statement? Or in the alternative, can you respond to the question of whether you believe a right to privacy protects a woman's choice to terminate her pregnancy?

KAVANAUGH: So I have not articulated a position on that. And consistent with the principle articulated, the nominee precedent that I feel duty-bound to follow as a matter of judicial independence, none of the seven other justices of—when they were nominees—have talked about that, nor about Heller, nor about Citizens United, nor about Lopez v. United States, Thurgood Marshall, about Miranda, Justice Brennan asked about . . .

HARRIS: Respectfully, Judge, as it relates to this hearing, you're not answering that question, and we can move on.

Can you think of any laws that give government the power to make decisions about the male body?

[Five second pause with dead silence]

KAVANAUGH: Uh. [Two Second Pause] I'm happy to answer a more specific question. But . . .

HARRIS: Male versus female.

KAVANAUGH: There are medical procedures. (grimacing)

HARRIS: That the government—that the government has the power to make a decision about a man's body?

KAVANAUGH: Thought you were asking about medical procedures that are unique to men. (flustered smile)

HARRIS: I'll repeat the question. Can you think of any laws that give the government the power to make decisions about the male body?

KAVANAUGH: I'm not—I'm not uh—I'm not thinking of any right now, Senator.[12]

Once again, Kamala Harris's command of the stage at a senate committee hearing was masterful, and Judge Kavanaugh's awkward silences and pained expressions became the top takeaway from the first two days of his senate confirmation hearings.

"Just everyone else leave and let Kamala Harris sit in the room with Kavanaugh and televise it," wrote author Amy Siskind in a viral tweet about the hearing.[13] "@SenKamalaHarris correctly explains the Ginsburg standard to Judge Kavanaugh—answering fair questions about women's constitutional rights and acknowledging previous writings," wrote Senate Democratic leadership in a viral video tweet about the exchange. "Judge Kavanaugh refuses to own his past writings or answer fair questions."[14]

"Kamala Harris and Cory Booker Have Upended the Kavanaugh Hearings," blared the headline in *Rolling Stone* magazine.[15] J. D. Durkin, a news host for the digital television station Cheddar, shared this anecdote on Twitter about the reaction to Senator Harris's sharp questions:

> [A] woman in my family—who has supported Trump since day 1 and defended him vigorously over the Access Hollywood tape—just texted me about Sen. Kamala Harris in the Kavanaugh hearings.
>
> "Freaking unreal! I love her."
> Would you vote for her over POTUS?
> "Yes! in any minute."[16]

The following night, Senator Harris got her answer from Judge Kavanaugh about his discussions with lawyers from the firm representing Trump. It wasn't a fully satisfying experience. She explained to MSNBC's Rachel Maddow why she asked those questions in a live television interview from inside a room deep inside the Senate chambers:

> MADDOW: You said that you have a lot you received reliable information that this nominee had at least one conversation with people at a law firm that is representing the president and then at one point represented the president in the Mueller investigation and that conversation

was specifically about Mueller and his probe. What do you make of the nominee giving you a sort of flat denial on that at last tonight?

HARRIS: Well I—you know, I frankly don't know why it took twenty-four hours to get a final answer that was a firm "no."

I'll tell you that, you know, he has been unable to agree that he should recuse themselves on the investigations if they should arrive at the Supreme Court and he were confirmed. He has not given clear answers on the special counsel in terms of whether the president can fire him and there`s, you know, a lot I think that has been about this thing where he's just been an evasive in terms of his answers.

MADDOW: He was really pressing you both last night and tonight to tell him who exactly you were asking about? Republicans suggested and the nominee himself suggested a little bit that that was the only way he could answer the question because he wouldn't have any way of knowing if people he was talking to about the investigation were in fact associated with that firm.

What did you make of that that framing in that effort to try to talk you out of that line of questioning?

HARRIS: I still—I must admit to you, Rachel, I`m still really unsure about why he keeps equivocating because you're absolutely right, he wanted clarification about who

> *exactly at the firm? He wanted, you know, a list of the*
> *people who are at the firm. He wanted to know what is*
> *the subject matter. You noticed even tonight he did that.*
>
> *And it leads me to believe that there's more to this*
> *than he's letting on, and I frankly that that when we look*
> *at his whole record, there's a lot about his record doing*
> *that should leave us with a lot of questions.*[17]

"The American public has a right to know that if certain matters go before the United States Supreme Court involving this president, that they'll be heard by [an impartial] justice in Supreme Court . . . ," the senator concluded.[18]

The following week, a bombshell revelation rocked Congress when Palo Alto University professor Christine Blasey Ford stepped forward with allegations of attempted sexual assault at the hands of Judge Kavanaugh when they were both teenagers growing up in suburban Maryland. She described in detail fearing for her life during their simultaneous teenage visit to a friend's house where Ford says Kavanaugh was "stumbling drunk" and held her down, then attempted to forcibly rape her until his best friend Mark Judge entered the room, jumping on them and ending the incident.[19] Harris supported Ford's right to be heard and called for an immediate FBI investigation into the incident on national television, explaining to *CBS This Morning*:

> *I want to know about this guy's background and the*
> *American public wants to know, are we about to put*
> *someone on the United States Supreme Court who com-*
> *mitted a sexual assault? The American public deserves to*

know the character of someone who will serve for his entire life on the highest court in our country.

I believe that the FBI should be compelled to do its job in terms of completing their background investigation and that's not being done.[20]

Ford's accusations against Kavanaugh were devastating to his nomination. Had the majority leader of the GOP-controlled Senate, Mitch McConnell (R-KY) not tossed out hundreds of years' worth of precedent to turn Supreme Court nominations into a simple majority vote, Kavanaugh wouldn't have been confirmed at that point. But because Republicans controlled the Senate and desperately wanted a highly partisan judge on the nation's top court, they pressed forward with the nomination. Judge Kavanaugh turned to partisan news outlet Fox News to make his case to Republicans that they should ignore all of the allegations, disclaiming any prior association with Ford.[21] The Fox appearance sparked judicial misconduct complaints against Kavanaugh by the Democratic Coalition and others for compromising the very judicial independence he repeatedly cited as a reason not to answer most of the senators' substantive questions.[22, 23] The judge released his calendars from high school before the hearing, but after Ford had told her story, in an attempt to clear his name.

Three days later, Judge Kavanaugh appeared for another hearing on September 27, 2018, and read a prepared statement alleging a partisan conspiracy theory with zero basis in fact naming the Clinton family as the source of Ford's sex assault allegations against him. It was a shocking moment, exposing Kavanaugh's partisan extremist viewpoint, upon which Senator

Harris's renewed questioning put the man to utter shame. It was clear where Senator Harris stood from her opening statement during questioning of Ford:

> *Dr. Ford, first of all, just so we can level set, you know you are not on trial. You are not on trial. You are sitting here before members of the United States Senate's Judiciary Committee because you had the courage to come forward, because, as you have said, you believe it was your civic duty. I was struck in your testimony by what you indicated as your intention when you first let anyone associated with these hearings know about it. And what you basically said is you reached out to your Representative in the United States Congress hoping that person would inform the white house before Judge Kavanaugh had been named. That's extremely persuasive about your motivation for coming forward.*
>
> *You have bravely come forward. And I want to thank you because you clearly have nothing to gain for what you have done. You have been a true patriot in fighting for the best of who we are as a country. I believe you are doing that because you love this country, and I believe history will show that you are a true profile in courage at this moment in time in the history of our country and I thank you.*[24]

Harris repeatedly asked Kavanaugh if he would call for an FBI investigation into his past conduct, which he repeatedly ducked, and she called him out on it. In their final exchange, she used logic and reason to completely tear down the judge's conspiracy theory:

HARRIS: You have said in your opening statement, you characterized these allegations as a conspiracy directed against you. I'll point out to you that Judge—Justice now, Neil Gorsuch was nominated by this president.

He was considered by this body, just last year. I did a rough kind of analysis of similarities—you both attended Georgetown Prep, you both attended very prestigious law schools, you both clerked for Justice Kennedy, you were both circuit judges, you were both nominated to the Supreme Court, you were both questioned about your record—the only difference is that you have been accused of sexual assault.

How do you reconcile your statement about a conspiracy against you with the treatment of someone who was before this body not very long ago?

KAVANAUGH: I explained that in my opening statement, Senator. Look at the evidence here, the calendars, look at the witness statements, look at Ms. Keyser's statement.

HARRIS: OK. And then, do you agree that it is possible for men to both be friends with some women, and treat other women badly?

KAVANAUGH: Of course, but the point I've been empha- sizing and that is if you go back to age 14 for me—you will find people, and not just people, lots of people who I've been friends with. Some of whom are in this room today, starting at age fourteen, women. And who've talked about my friendships with them through my whole life, and it's a consistent pattern all the way through.

Sixty-five women, who knew me more than thirty-five years ago, signed a letter to support me after the allegation was made because they know me, and they were with me, and we grew up together, we talked on the phone together and we went to events together. That is who I am.

What the people who worked with me in the Bush White House, the—the women there, look at what Sarah Day said in CentralMaine.com. Look at the—what the law clerks—I have sent more women law clerks to the Supreme Court than any other federal judge in the country.

HARRIS: I only have a few seconds left and I'll just ask you a direct question. Did you watch Dr. Ford's testimony?

KAVANAUGH: I did not. I plan to . . . [25]

Amazingly, the very calendar that Kavanaugh released intending to clear his name wound up circumstantially implicating him in Ford's allegations, which she made before seeing the document.[26] A thinly veiled fictional book by Kavanaugh's best friend Judge about Georgetown Prep also confirmed Ford's time line.[27] Senate Republicans had brought in an Arizona prosecutor to question both Kavanaugh and Ford, and when she began piecing together Kavanaugh's calendar, they shut her down, replacing thoughtful questions with angry diatribes.[28] Despite the entirely credible allegations against Judge Kavanaugh, Senate Republicans voted his nomination out of committee on a party line vote. However, they did so under the stipulation that the final vote would be delayed for a week for the FBI to investigate Ford's allegations.[29] The limited FBI investigation was not able to prove Kavanaugh committed the crime, and he was confirmed to the Supreme Court.

"This should have been a search for the truth," said Harris on the Senate floor, thundering her opposition to Kavanaugh's nomination on October 5, 2018. "They should have been allowed to do their full job. But instead the White House did not allow it. This was not a search for the truth. Instead, this was about politics and raw power to push through an unfit nominee."[30] Kavanaugh was confirmed in a vote along party lines 50–48, the smallest margin to confirm a Supreme Court justice in modern American history.[31]

The impact on Kamala Harris's political career was immediate. She had been preparing a presidential run already, but the weekend following Kavanaugh's nomination on a campaign swing in Ohio, Harris came face-to-face with throngs of new fans who appreciated her holding Judge Kavanaugh's feet to the fire for every moment of his nomination process. *Politico* reported:

> Harris's reception here laid bare the timely opening that Kavanaugh's confirmation appears to provide for the junior senator from California. On Sunday, Ohio Sen. Sherrod Brown, himself a potential 2020 candidate, thanked her publicly for her "courage" and "how you led the way in those hearings."

At a rally earlier Sunday, a crowd roared for Harris when Brown asked rhetorically, "Did she kick ass on the Senate Judiciary Committee?"

When Harris asked Kavanaugh in a committee hearing if he could think of any laws that "give the government the power to make decisions about the male body," said Sandy Theis, a Democratic consultant and former executive director of Progress Ohio said, "Ohio cheered." "That's when I started to hear people really talk about what a badass she is," Theis said.

Harris is expected to visit Iowa before the November elections. But on Sunday, surrounded by thickets of supporters in Ohio, she hugged activists, posed for selfies and signed photographs and campaign signs. When Harris began to explain why she had come to the state, a rally-goer called out, "running for president!" and the crowd erupted in cheers.

Harris told reporters that in the wake of the Kavanaugh hearings, her "biggest fear is that there will be a group of people who retreat, right? That's my biggest fear, that there will be people who will decide that if they speak out it doesn't matter, and will feel deflated by what happened in a way that causes them to recede." She said, "That's part of why I'm here today: to remind people that their voices really do matter, and they have to speak, and speak out and speak up and that they matter."

Two days after her visit to Ohio, Senator Harris's tough questions about the FBI's background investigation of Justice Kavanaugh made national headlines *again*, when she got Director Christopher Wray to admit that the White House had limited the scope of his agency's background investigation into Christine Blasey Ford's allegations.[32] It was a fitting denouement to the Kavanaugh hearings, proving perfectly how Republicans in the White House and Senate were not interested in their nominee's background or character, just his partisan loyalty. Harris has "cult star status in Iowa after the Kavanaugh hearings" at the end of October 2018, according to *Buzzfeed News,* which led the junior senator from California to having the kind of problems that presidential candidates dream of having:

> On her first visit to Iowa as a potential presidential candidate, Sen. Kamala Harris developed a problem with doors: She couldn't get out of them. She barely finished a speech before she was swarmed, admirers blocking all exits, asking for photographs or looking for conversations with the senator.
>
> There was a certain look people got as they left the crowds that formed around Harris: flushed and giddy, some gushing about what the California senator had just told them. In Ankeny on Monday, a college student left the crowd with tears in her eyes after a conversation with Harris about her rape and the importance of fighting back after the confirmation of Supreme Court Justice Brett Kavanaugh.
>
> As much as Harris drew comparisons to Barack Obama in Iowa, her supporters also couldn't help but compare

her to Hillary Clinton, who some said they'd seen speak in the years running up to her two losing presidential campaigns.

"Hillary was good one-on-one, but [Harris] connects with everyone," said Gwendolyn Kingsbury, an accountant in Indianola. "She's a powerful woman—she sucks you in. She just has this natural ability to connect with people."

Many of the Iowans who turned out for Harris said they had first encountered her on cable news and social media. But it was the Kavanaugh hearings, they said, that epitomized what many saw as one of Harris' best qualities: strength.

"She was very strong," said Myskal Kanietova, an accountant in Des Moines. "She can stay strong and be herself by staying dignified. Someone comes at her, and she has very strong comebacks."[33]

The reporter noted that her name recognition was best among news junkies, but that's who a presidential candidate needs to impact in order to staff a campaign, get donations, and win a party primary in the first state, Iowa. She wasn't the only senator looking to make a splash at the Kavanaugh hearings, but she drew out the most crucial issues in her questioning compared to her colleagues, Senator Cory Booker and Senator Amy Klobuchar. While the others both fought hard to prevent Kavanaugh's nomination, neither impacted public opinion in quite the same way.

The following year, Christine Blasey Ford was chosen as one of *Time* magazine's TIME 100: The Most Influential People of 2019 for her bravery to speak out about sexual assault in the U.S. Senate. Kamala Harris wrote her introduction:

> *Her story, spoken while holding back tears, shook Washington and the country. Her courage, in the face of those who wished to silence her, galvanized Americans. And her unfathomable sacrifice, out of a sense of civic duty, shined a spotlight on the way we treat survivors of sexual violence.*
>
> *Christine Blasey Ford's ambition wasn't to become a household name or make it onto this list. She had a good life and a successful career—and risked everything to send a warning in a moment of grave consequence.*
>
> *At her core, she is a teacher. And through her courage, she forced the country to reckon with an issue that has too often been ignored and kept in the dark.*[34]

Senator Harris spoke for all Democrats frustrated with the results of the Kavanaugh hearings, in which Republicans rushed through a partisan nominee, who had been credibly accused of sexual assault because the Senate Majority Leader believed that was a great idea politically to connect with his party's base.[35] Harris's deft questioning pointed out sharp differences with the Republican party on everything from abortion to race relations to Russian election interference. In the process, Harris burnished her national reputation as a fighter for justice, a fighter for women's rights and racial equality, and for being respectfully tough under the biggest spotlight.

CAMPAIGN PLATFORM

Senator Kamala Harris has not published a campaign issues website page or created a policy agenda as of April 2019, but she has submitted bills to Congress which tell a story about her policy preferences. In addition, she has discussed her domestic policy ideas in town hall forums, but she has not fleshed out a detailed foreign policy position, paper, or speech as of late April 2019.

Harris has announced a major tax cut plan for the middle-class that is the same size as the GOP's 2017 tax cut to the wealthiest 1 percent of Americans and the country's largest corporations. It's similar to a universal basic income program. The first major policy announcement in her 2020 Democratic policy campaign is a significant plan to raise teacher pay across the country. She has also announced that if elected, she would take major action on gun reform in her first hundred days if Congress doesn't act, and the California senator is a supporter of Medicare for All to bring universal health care to America.

Senator Harris's liberal ideology is very much in line with the mainstream of Democratic Party thinking in California, the country's most progressive state, which means she wants to extend the social safety net to promote a better life for regular people who earn less. Harris wants to institute a plan that will cushion the financial blow to renters forced to pay large shares of their income for rent. However, the senator has told early-state crowds that she should not be pegged in any fixed ideological category.[1] As a former prosecutor, Harris is a bipartisan advocate for criminal justice reform and wants to reform immigration. She is also a prominent supporter of the Green New Deal and fighting climate change.

Her career as a prosecutor was marked by a reliance on data over anecdotes, which led to her signature book *Smart on Crime*, a volume that concentrated on busting myths with facts. It was a parallel to her opponent Senator Elizabeth Warren's (D-MA) writing a book dismissing myths about bankruptcy and replacing them with factual stories based on data.

The senator's early campaign is heavily based on her personal narrative and her reliably progressive responses to the many issues of the day, though she is quick to suggest a study or follow-up as a rhetorical parry when she doesn't support an issue rather than flatly decline to support something she is asked about but not in favor of doing.

LIFT THE MIDDLE CLASS ACT

Kamala Harris's top initiative as a presidential candidate is her plan to lift millions of children and their working poor families out of poverty by a vast expansion of the Earned Income Tax Credit (EITC).[2] The EITC was enacted in 1975 as a supplement to working people as an alternative to welfare payments, but it wasn't available to the childless working poor and didn't vary based on household size.[3]

A major bipartisan update to the EITC passed in 1993, which President Clinton wanted to expand in 2000, noting on the White House website that it lifted 2.3 million American children out of poverty in the seven preceding years.[4] In 2009, the American Reinvestment and Recovery Act, best known as the Obama stimulus plan, expanded the EITC again for families with more than three children.[5] *The Atlantic* wrote about Senator Harris's plan to expand the EITC:

> *Harris is offering a kind of fun-house-mirror inversion of the sweeping Republican tax initiative, one that would, instead of slashing rates on high-income households and corporations, push huge credits out to middle-income and poor families. The lift the Middle Class Act would provide monthly cash payments of up to $500 to lower-income families, on top of the tax credits and public benefits they already receive. "Last year, Congress gave a trillion dollars in tax breaks to corporations," Harris told me. "That money should have gone to American taxpayers who need it instead of handing it over to corporations and the top 1 percent."*

Harris is offering as much as $3,000 a year for a single person or $6,000 a year for a married couple, on top of existing tax and transfer programs, disbursed either as a lump-sum tax refund or as a monthly payment. Working families making less than $100,000 a year would qualify, including those making close to nothing. As many as 80 million Americans would benefit, Harris's office has estimated, with the Center on Budget and Policy Priorities calculating that the proposal would lift 9 million people out of poverty, including nearly 3 million kids.[6]

The Harris plan would stimulate the economy by providing funds to people most likely to spend the money, unlike tax cuts to wealthy persons, who are more likely to invest a tax cut. America spends one of the smallest shares of its national GDP on anti-poverty programs of any major industrialized nation, and it's no wonder that the nonpartisan Economic Policy Institute finds that our country has a very high childhood poverty rate relative to those nations.[7]

The Tax Policy Center notes that Harris's plan would pay for itself by repealing the vast benefits flowing to taxpayers who earn more than $100,000 favored by the GOP's 2017 Tax Cuts and Jobs Act.[8]

EDUCATION POLICY

Kamala Harris has a pair of education proposals aimed at helping habitually underpaid teachers across the country to earn a fair salary and making college affordable for every eligible student. The senator's plan would create a federal funding formula to support more than 85 percent of the proposed pay increases with some funding from local sources. She introduced the plan in Houston, Texas, at the end of March 2019, CNN reports:

> *Introducing a bold campaign promise—aimed squarely at women and people of color, her target zone for voters—the California Democrat pledged to make the largest federal investment in history toward teacher salaries, which would close the wage gap between teachers and similar professionals, by the end of her first term.*

According to a CNN review of the policy proposal, released by the campaign Tuesday morning, Harris has pledged to provide teachers with an average raise of $13,500, which would amount to a 23 percent average increase in salary. The plan would cost approximately $315 billion over 10 years, according to the outline of the policy.[9]

The goal of Harris's plan would be to make up the 11 percent gap between teacher pay and the average pay of other college graduates.[10] She would pay for it by expanding the estate tax and other taxes on the top 1 percent of taxpayers.

"In fact, a teacher pay raise will pay for itself. No—actually, raising teacher pay will likely make money for the government," wrote UC Santa Barbara economics professor Dick Startz about Harris's plan in *Newsday*:

It's well established that an extra year of student learning raises lifetime earnings by about 10 percent. We can also work out roughly how much more students would learn from better-paid teachers. A Columbia University study looking across states finds that a raise of the size Harris proposes would have a measurable impact: On average, graduating students would have gained the equivalent of an extra 30 percent of a school year. International comparisons of teacher salaries and student performance suggest an effect three times that size.

Even if we take the lower figure, that would create a 3 percent increase in overall earnings. Labor income in the United States is about $13.3 trillion, so 3 percent of that is $400 billion dollars a year.

Americans pay an average federal income tax of 14 percent (leaving out sales and other taxes), so these increased wages would produce $56 billion in annual tax revenue —almost twice the cost of Harris's program. That not only pays for the teacher raises, it leaves plenty of spare change.[11]

The American Federation of Teachers is a backer of Harris's plan to raise teacher salaries. "This is an issue in all communities," says AFT president Randi Weingarten. "It is a woman's issue. It affects people of color. These issues of education and health care are front and center in this election."[12]

Kamala Harris is a backer of the Sanders "College for All" plan, telling a student audience about her policy ideas during an April 2019 CNN town hall event:

I do support debt-free college. I also believe that what we need to do is we need to allow students to refinance your student loan debt.

And in particular, I'm supporting an initiative that would allow you to refinance your student loan debt such that it would be on par with the federal lending amounts.

> *So, for example, if you—probably none of you here, but any of your older brothers and sisters, if you took out student loans between the years of about 2006 through 2013, the interest rate was about 7 percent. What I am proposing is, regardless of the interest rate at the time that you took out your student loans, that upon repayment it would have to be at 3.5 percent. . . . Part of the issue is that terms of repayment, there is no connection between what you owe and your income. So what I would be requiring is that there be a robust process by which income-based repayment would be the norm.*

"College has become a dream that is weighed down with a giant price tag that an individual could only imagine taking on," wrote Senator Harris on *Medium* in April 2017.[13] "Those who take that challenge face mountains of debt and are trapped in a devastating cycle of loans that will follow them for decades."

GUN REFORM

Senator Harris's campaign has said that she wants to make gun trafficking a federal crime, ban high-capacity magazines, and forbid anyone convicted of a federal hate crime from owning a gun.[14] However, she made a tremendous splash during an April 2019 televised town hall on CNN in Manchester, New Hampshire, saying:

Upon being elected, I will give the United States Congress 100 days to get their act together and have the Courage to pass reasonable gun safety laws. And if they fail to do it, then I will take executive action.

And specifically what I will do is put in place a requirement that for anyone who sells more than five guns a year, they are required to do background checks when they sell those guns. I will require that for any gun dealer that breaks the law, the ATF take their license. And by the way, ATF, alcohol, tobacco and firearms, well, the ATF has been doing a lot of the "A" and the "T," but not much of the "F." And we need to fix that.

And then—on the third piece, because none of us have been sleeping over the last two years, part of what has happened under the current administration is they took fugitives off the list of prohibited people. I'd put them back on the list, meaning that fugitives from justice should not be able to purchase a handgun or any kind of weapon. So that's what I'd do.[15]

Harris rejects the "false choice" of extremist NRA and Republican talking points against taking action against unsafe gun ownership or doing nothing about guns.

MEDICARE FOR ALL

Kamala Harris is a leading advocate for universal health care. She used her platform as California's attorney general to defend the Affordable Care Act, which guarantees universal health policy issuance by private companies, regardless of preexisting conditions.

Senator Harris cosponsored her now-Democratic 2020 primary opponent's Sen. Bernie Sanders's (D-VT) 2017 Medicare for All Act, alongside her other opponents Senators Warren, Kirsten Gillibrand (D-NY), and Cory Booker (D-NJ).[16] She continued her support along that same cast of colleagues when Senator Sanders reintroduced his Medicare for All Act in April 2019.[17]

The key feature of Medicare for All is that it will eliminate the private market for primary health insurance policies within about four years. However, the California senator explained what that really means to CNN's Don Lemon better than any other candidate in the race at a recent town hall event:

> On the issue of this whole dynamic about access to private insurance, of course, private insurance, you can get supplemental insurance . . .
>
> But let's not be duped by a messaging campaign that has been waged for years by the insurance companies to have you into believing that you need to defend them. You need to defend yourself.
>
> You know what? Ninety-one percent of the doctors are in Medicare. So the idea and the suggestion they're trying to make to you is really a false one. You will be able

> *to have your doctor. Ninety-one percent of them are in*
> *the Medicare system.*[18]

Kamala Harris spent her teenage years living in Canada with her mother, a cancer researcher, so she learned what a universal health care system looks like and how it works, which may make her the best positioned candidate to explain it in the 2020 Democratic primary field. In Canada, they spend about half as much per capita as Americans for full coverage, and supplemental health insurance policies amount to 12 percent of that spending, a little over $45 billion annually.[19, 20]

RENT RELIEF

Senator Harris is the primary sponsor of the Rent Relief Act, a federal bill she rolled out in July 2018 that would provide housing assistance to millions of Americans paying more than 30 percent of their incomes toward rents. Mortgage holders have enjoyed decades of federal subsidies in the form of tax preferences like the interest deduction and property tax deductions, but renters are generally left out of the picture even though there is no major push to enable the 35.6 percent of Americans who do not own their own homes to purchase property.

Kamala Harris plan would provide a 100 percent rent subsidy to the lowest-income families, effectively replacing HUD's Section 8 program with a tax program instead. California's senior senator and Democrats in Connecticut and New Hampshire cosponsored her bill.[21] "America's affordable housing crisis has left too many families behind who struggle each month to keep a roof over their head. This bill will ensure no family is priced out of the basic security of a place to live. Bolstering the economic security of working families would strengthen our country and increase opportunity," she said in a press release. The mayors of Los Angeles, Oakland, Sacramento, and Stockton, California, all endorsed her bill.

Critics believe that Harris's proposal to subsidize rents during an affordable housing shortage would artificially drive up prices, comparing it to student loans, and claim that the program would cause rent increases because tenants don't care to shop for housing.[22] However, they fail to take into account the difference between the two markets, since student borrowing is not a basic necessity and housing is one which nearly 100 percent of Americans already consume. Furthermore, rental increases of 3–4 percent annually on residential rental property are the norm due to ever-rising inflation, property taxes, and insurance costs.

"Housing is a human right, and we must act now to end the affordable housing crisis and provide relief to working families who are worried about making each month's rent," said Harris when she reintroduced the Senate bill in April 2019, which gained a House companion bill sponsored by representatives from Illinois and California.[23] "Right now, nearly half of Americans couldn't afford an emergency $400 expense—these families need help now. This is about more than just economics—it's about the basic security and dignity that every American deserves to have in their own home."

BIPARTISAN BAIL-REFORM EFFORTS

Senator Harris coauthored the Pretrial Safety and Integrity Act of 2017 with Senator Rand Paul (R-KY), a bill that would assist 600,000 Americans forced to await jail in trial for lack of resources to post cash bail.[24]

"Too many people in this country must spend weeks, months, or even years in jail waiting for trial only because they can't afford bail," said the ACLU's legislative counsel Kanya Bennett about the bill.[25] "Even though these people are innocent in the eyes of the law, they're punished, deprived of their freedom with disastrous consequences for their families and their lives. While this bill isn't perfect, its reforms would be progress towards fixing the systematic problems that have led to mass incarceration." The two senators coauthored a *New York Times* op-ed about the bill, explaining:

> Instead of the federal government mandating a one-size-fits-all approach, this bill provides Department of Justice grants directly to the states so each can devise and carry out the most effective policies, tailored for its unique needs. Enabling states to better institute such reforms also honors one of our nation's core documents, the Bill of Rights. In drafting the Eighth Amendment, which prohibits excessive bail, the founders sought to protect people from unchecked government power in the criminal justice system.
>
> First, our legislation empowers states to build on best practices. Kentucky and New Jersey, for instance, have shifted from bail toward personalized risk assessments that analyze factors such as criminal history and substance abuse. These are better indicators of whether a defendant is a flight risk or a threat to the public and

ought to be held without bail. Colorado and West Virginia have improved pretrial services and supervision, such as using telephone reminders so fewer defendants miss court dates and end up detained.

These nudges work. Over the second half of 2006, automated phone call reminders in Multnomah County in Oregon, resulted in 750 people showing up in court who otherwise may have forgotten their date.[26]

She has also introduced other civil rights and criminal justice reform items while in the Senate, including the Justice of Victims of Lynching Act and the Do No Harm Act. The former would make it a federal crime to lynch another person—a form of vigilantism racists practiced in the South to murder African Americans—with new penalties of up to ten years in prison. The anti-lynching legislation—which has sixteen Republican sponsors—passed the Senate at the end of 2018 in bipartisan fashion, and has been reauthorized by a voice vote in 2019, where it awaits action by the House.[27, 28] There is a good chance it will become law.

The Do No Harm Act would amend the Religious Freedom Restoration Act, a federal law often invoked by bigots to violate the civil rights of others, to ensure that the civil rights of LGBT people and others are respected.[29]

IMMIGRATION STANCE

As the daughter of immigrants, Kamala Harris sees herself as a protector of those who come to America, and her policy ideas show it. She is a cosponsor of the REUNITE Act, which would do just that for the thousands of refugee children the Trump administration separated from their parents at the southern border without a plan to care for them.

"This is a crisis created by this administration and has resulted in thousands of children being ripped from their mothers and fathers," said Sen. Harris, whose cosponsors were Nevada Senator Cortez Masto and Oregon Senator Jeff Merkley. "Government should be in the business of keeping families together not tearing them apart. A stunning lack of transparency and accountability has left thousands of children in need of reunification. That must happen immediately.

"We are better than this."[30]

Senator Harris has sparred with the head of the Department of Homeland Security frequently in public hearings, as well as Trump's failed nominee to lead the bureau of Immigration and Customs Enforcement.

GREEN NEW DEAL AND CLIMATE CHANGE

Senator Harris's positions on climate change and the Green New Deal are very mainstream in her home state of California and among progressive thinkers. She explained why she's a supporter of combating climate change to a skeptical student during a springtime town hall event broadcast on CNN with Don Lemon:

> QUESTION: The Green New Deal is not a law but rather a memorandum that has no actual legislative effect. It's been characterized as expensive, divides Democrats, and

has no chance of passing through Congress in its current state. Why do you support it?

HARRIS: I support it because I, to my core, know that the climate crisis is representing an existential threat to who we are as human beings. We have had supposed leaders who are buying—and pushing science fiction instead of science fact, and this is to our collective peril if we don't take this matter seriously with a sense of urgency.

Why I support the Green New Deal is because it does that. It puts timelines in effect. It appreciates that we need to take this seriously and the clock is ticking every day on this issue, and every day we fail to act will be to our collective consequence. The U.N. has already said over the next twelve years if we don't get this straight there will be severe consequence. And this is within our ability to do something about it. Listen . . . families are impacted by this. You know, children, seniors, we all need to . . . drink clean water and breathe clean air.[31]

Harris explained that America's farmers in the Midwest and firefighters in California are all suffering under the ill effects of rising temperatures from climate change, and detailed how reorienting our economy away from carbon pollution will create millions of new jobs.

"The greatest thing about [the Green New Deal] that I am really enjoying, it is causing these conversations to happen around our country in a way they've not been in the last few years, and hopefully everyone is understanding that so much of the harm we are doing to our planet is caused by us as human beings," the senator concluded about the New York Representative Alexandria Ocasio-Cortez's plan, after explaining that her goal is to bring California's economic miracle to the rest of the country.[32] "And the solutions will be because we change our behaviors without much requirement of change to lifestyle, and it will be urgent in terms of the work we need to do and the approach we need to have."

OTHER POLICY ISSUES

Senator Harris has not published any web pages on foreign policy, hasn't made any major speeches on foreign policy, and hasn't taken any major public stances on foreign policy, aside from her strong stance against foreign election interference. Harris serves on the Senate Intelligence Committee and participated in the investigation into Russia's election interference to assist the Trump campaign in 2016. Other than that, she will have to elucidate a foreign policy platform as the 2020 Democratic primary plan unfolds.

Harris has made support for historically black colleges and universities a point. "Being a proud member and graduate of an HBCU, Howard University, and what we need to do to support our HBCUs," she explained to CNN's Don Lemon explaining her plan to assist historically black upper education institutions. "I had a piece of legislation that actually has been passed to invest federal resources in supporting our HBCUs, recognizing that HBCUs really produce in some professions the majority of African Americans who enter those professions."

Indeed, her bill to reauthorize funding for the historic preservation program at HBCUs passed the Senate in February 2019 and became law as part of a larger bill sponsored by Sen. Lisa Murkowski (R-AK) a month later.[33, 34] It is always a big accomplishment to pass a bill in Congress and make it become law, but it is a tremendous feat to do so with bipartisan support in a legislative minority and get a president from the opposing party to sign it into law. It will help the schools with funds for capital improvements to their aging educational facilities.

Senator Harris supports a woman's right to make decisions about her own body, tweeting after she voted against a twenty-week abortion ban bill, "Senate GOP's proposed 20-week abortion ban is another example of politicians playing politics with health care. #NoAbortionBan."[35] Recently, she told *The Root* that she supports decriminalizing consensual sex work, though she has been a strong supporter of efforts to close down backpage.com, as discussed in Chapter 7.[36]

Harris's stances on other issues regularly hew to Democratic Party lines. She is in favor of opening a national conversation about slavery reparations, which is in line with the left wing of the Democratic Party's policies of fighting discrimination in its many forms.

Kamala Harris's policies put her squarely in the Democratic field's left wing, which is a territory that is dominated in the polls early by Vermont Senator Bernie Sanders and sought by Senators Elizabeth Warren and Gillibrand, as well as up-and-coming South Bend, Indiana, mayor Pete Buttigieg. Harris is well to the left of former vice president Joe Biden and Senator Amy Klobuchar, who are aiming for the party's moderate wing of voters.

The senator will draw her greatest contrast with progressive opponents like Sanders and Warren with her law enforcement background and rhetorical skills, as well as her targeted efforts to help renters and teachers, two very large likely blocs of primary voters.

Harris will likely stress the boldness of her domestic policy plans to correct income inequality when debating her adversaries in the moderate and centrist wing of the Democratic primary, such as Joe Biden or Senator Cory Booker (NJ), who is more aligned with the corporate wing of the Democratic Party.

Senator Harris has not presented her comprehensive set of domestic policies as an agenda or platform yet, but there is a lot of substance in her response to the major problems impacting every American. It will be a political challenge to distill her disparate policies into a single platform that is easy for the average person to digest and attracts the average Democratic primary voter. She will also need to find a way to make her platform appetizing to moderate and centrist independent voters, because that's the only way she will be able to defeat an eventual Republican candidate in the November 3, 2020, general election.

FORMATIVE BACKGROUND AND EDUCATION

Kamala Devi Harris's rapid rise from San Francisco district attorney to Washington, DC, began in Oakland, California, where she was born in 1964 to highly educated immigrant parents from Jamaica and India. Her mother, Shyamala Gopalan Harris, emigrated to America from Chennai in southern India as a nineteen-year-old college student at the University of California, Berkeley, and became a breast cancer researcher and civil rights activist before passing away at age seventy in 2009, of breast cancer.[1] Kamala Harris's father, Donald J. Harris, emigrated from Jamaica to attend the same school one year after her mother arrived in 1960. Both earned doctorate degrees.

"My parents were very active in the civil rights movement," said Harris on ABC's *Good Morning America* during her campaign launch on January 21, 2019, the morning of Martin Luther King Jr. Day.[2] "And it was about a belief that we are a country that was founded on noble ideals, and that we are at our best when we fight for those ideals. The thing about Dr. King that also inspires me is that he was aspirational. He was aspirational like our country is aspirational. We know that we've not yet reached those ideals, but our strength is that we fight to reach those ideals."

However, Kamala's parents split when she was five years old and divorced when she was eight, right before her father became a tenured professor of economics at Stanford University in 1972; he later retired as professor emeritus in 1998.[3, 4] She was raised in both the Hindu and the Baptist faiths.[5] Visiting India every two years with her family introduced young Kamala to her grandfather, P. V. Gopalan. He was an Indian diplomat whose government experience began the country's freedom from colonial status and ended with him in an office equivalent to a deputy secretary of state.[6]

At the age of twelve, Harris, her mother, and her sister, Maya Harris, who is two years younger, all moved to Montreal so her mother could work at the prestigious McGill University in French-speaking Quebec, Canada. "The thought of moving away from sunny California in February, in the middle of the school year, to a French-speaking foreign city covered in 12 feet of snow was distressing, to say the least," she wrote in her campaign autobiography *The Truths We Hold: An American Journey*.[7] As Canadian television network CTV noted, Kamala Harris adapted to her mother's career move:

> At the age of 13, Harris organized a protest in front of the building where she lived in Montreal because the owner didn't want children playing on the lawn, her sister Maya told *San Francisco Gate* in 2012. Harris convinced other children to join her in protesting and they convinced the building's owner to change the rule, according to the news site. That story doesn't surprise Trevor Williams,

who knew both the Harris sisters when they lived in Montreal and describes them as popular and studious.

"They always had the best grades in the class and everything seemed so easy for them," he told The Canadian Press. "But in reality, they succeeded because they worked hard, their mother was very strict. Often, when the rest of us went to the movies, the sisters had to stay home to study."

In a 1981 yearbook from Westmount High School, the then-16 year old Harris described her favourite pastime as "dancing with Midnight Magic," a dance troupe she founded with her friend Wanda Kagan. "We performed in community centres in front of elderly people or danced at fund-raisers," Kagan told The Canadian Press. "Outside of our studies, dance took up a lot of our time."[8]

In fact, the youthful protest described above involved sister Maya L. Harris as well, and it succeeded.[9] Both sisters credit their mother for instilling their values and their drive to succeed. Eventually, the future senator from California graduated from Westmount High School in 1981, and the school and its alumni are proud to have an alum in the 2020 presidential primary campaign.[10]

After graduation, Kamala Harris enrolled at Howard University, a historically black university[11] located in Washington, DC, only a couple of miles northeast of the White House. Recently, she spoke with the *Los Angeles Times* about her decision to return to the United States and attend the prestigious school, where she majored in political science and economics:

> *I reference often my days at Howard to help people understand they should not make assumptions about who black people are. My mother understood she was raising two black children to be black women. There was nothing unnatural or in conflict about it at all. There were a lot of kids at Howard who had a background where one parent was maybe from the Philippines and the other might be from Nairobi. Howard encompasses the diaspora.*[12]

Howard University is also where Harris won her first election to the Liberal Arts Student Council, no small feat in a school where the competition for student political office is legendarily fierce. Kamala Harris joined the Alpha Kappa Alpha sorority at Howard (which was founded there in 1908), a group of nearly 300,000 members across the nation, which CNN calls her "secret weapon" of supporters.[13] She graduated in 1986, and received the Outstanding Alumni Award from her alma mater in 2006 for her "work in the fields of law and public service."[14] After declaring herself a presidential candidate, Senator Harris made her first campaign appearance at Howard.[15]

After graduation, Harris returned to California and enrolled at the UC, Hastings College of the Law in San Francisco. She explained that decision to Super Lawyer in 2010 during her first campaign for California attorney general:

> *Because at the dinner table in my family, which always included extended family, there was always some*

passionate debate about something. And everyone, regardless of their age, was expected to defend, with logic, their positions. In that environment you couldn't help but develop skills because it was needed for survival. Also lawyers were the heroes of the civil rights movement. There was Thurgood Marshall and Charles Hamilton Houston and Constance Baker Motley. They used the skills of their profession to lead the passion from the streets into the courtrooms of this country.[16]

She graduated from UC Hastings with a juris doctor degree and joined the State Bar of California on June 14, 1990.[17]

A SISTER ACT

By serving as campaign chair, Maya Harris is destined to be one of the faces of her sister's campaign.

Kamala Harris's younger sister Maya is an accomplished lawyer and political strategist. She is a former vice president at the Ford Foundation and former senior fellow at the Center for American Progress think tank.[18] Maya Harris has also been an MSNBC on-air contributor, and she was one of only three senior policy advisers in the inner circle of Hillary Clinton's 2016 campaign.[19] Former Clinton campaign chairman John Podesta called her a "partner with Hillary" in developing a domestic agenda.[20]

When she was seventeen, Maya Harris became a single mother; by the age of twenty-nine she became one of the youngest law school deans in the country.[21] Maya graduated from Stanford Law School in 1992 while raising her young daughter, and she later married the president of its law review, Tony West.[22] West's twenty-seven-year law career took him to the prestigious role of associate attorney general for the final years of the Obama administration (the third-ranking official in the Department of Justice). Maya's husband Tony served as co-chair for Senator-elect Harris's transition team in 2016.[23]

While one sister worked in the Alameda County district attorney's office in Oakland, California, which Kamala joined as a prosecutor in 1990 and where she worked through 1998, the other sister headed a civil rights group named PolicyLink, then later the ACLU of Northern California. In 2001, Maya Harris issued a key 150-page report titled "Community-Centered Policing: A Force for Change" through PolicyLink which was the first major academic exposé revealing the wrongs of America's 1990s policies of mass incarceration.[24] Later, Maya would provide editorial feedback for *The New Jim Crow* by her Stanford classmate, Michelle Alexander, which is a seminal work in the new movement for civil rights that revealed the steady erosion of the constitution's Fourth Amendment by the courts in the service of America's failed drug war from the Nixon era to the present.[25]

Currently, Maya Harris's husband Tony West is Uber's corporate secretary, senior vice president, and general counsel. Her daughter Meena Harris became the campaign's head of strategy and leadership after graduating from Harvard Law School in 2012.[26]

Naturally, when Kamala Harris decided to run for president, she consulted with the person she knows the best in politics. According to *Talking Points Memo*, Maya Harris is "helping to shape Kamala's policy platform and political strategy, with an intense focus on nonwhite and female voters:

> *Those are the dominant groups in modern Democratic politics—and ones Maya has spent decades studying. Maya's former colleagues describe her as brilliant, driven and grounded. She has an explosive laugh that matches Kamala's, but a softer touch, and unassailable civil rights credentials that could help her prosecutor sister fend off mounting attacks from the left.*
>
> *"I definitely think there is a greater level of integrity in the way [the Harris sisters] conduct themselves, [but] you think back to John Kennedy and Bobby Kennedy as an example of a very political, intensely ambitious and thoughtful individuals," said Kate Kendall, a friend of Maya's and former head of the National Center for Lesbian Rights. "As siblings, the sum is greater than the parts."*[27]

Maya Harris has deep roots in the progressive movement and the civil rights arena. She also brings a level of national political experience to the job that few other campaigns out of Senator Harris's seventeen competitors will be able to match. While she is content to remain behind the scenes, May Harris's presence will likely emerge at some point of the 2020 Democratic primary.

A CAREER PROSECUTOR

Kamala Harris specialized in prosecuting violent crimes including rape, homicide, and child sex-assault cases at the Alameda County DA's office. It was that era when her name first hit the San Francisco newspapers because of her brief romantic involvement with one of the giants of California politics, Willie Brown, who was then speaker of the state assembly and went on to be mayor of San Francisco in 1996. The relationship fizzled before Brown's mayoral campaign began.[28] He would go on to appoint Harris to a pair of state boards, a full-time position on the California Unemployment Insurance Appeals Board—which required a six-month leave of absence from the district attorney's office—and then to the California Medical Assistance Commission just before the end of his Speakership, both which are paid positions with a six-figure salary in today's dollars.[29, 30]

In 1998, Harris moved to the San Francisco DA's office to be the managing attorney of their career criminal unit. She simultaneously held the position of chief of the San Francisco City Attorney's Division on Children and Families.[31] Then, at the recommendation of City Attorney Louise Renne, the San Francisco City attorney's office hired Harris full-time in 2000, and she served as its Co-Chief of the Community and Neighborhood Division, handling civil code enforcement matters.[32] That is also when she cofounded the Coalition to End the Exploitation of Kids and changed the prosecutorial focus from ending the selling of sex to helping women who have been trapped by addiction, domineering men, or financial distress to get out of a life of prostitution. It led to San Francisco's first "safe house" for women in the sex trade being opened.

But Harris believed that the San Francisco DA was politicizing the office and quit in 2000. Her campaign began right then to replace her former San Francisco City and County DA's office boss, DA Terence Hallinan.[33]

Harris's 2004 campaign bio also noted these other public service positions:

> *Co-Chair of the Lawyers' Committee for Civil Rights; President of the Board of Directors of Partners Ending Domestic Abuse; elected member of the Board of Directors of the San Francisco Bar Association; and founder of an SF Museum of Modern Art mentoring program which has served hundreds of young people from the inner city.*[34]

Harris ran for the office of San Francisco's district attorney in 2003 and beat her old boss, Hallinan, in a runoff by a whopping thirteen-point margin.[35] On Thursday, January 8, 2004 Chief Justice of the California Supreme Court Ronald M. George administered the oath of office to Harris.[36]

Seven years later, in 2010, Harris ran for statewide office for the first time and earned a historic victory to become California's attorney general. She married attorney Douglas Emhoff in 2014 after a successful blind date, and is stepmother to his two children, Cole and Ella, from a previous marriage.[37, 38] When Senator Barbara Boxer retired in 2016, Harris beat Rep. Loretta Sanchez (D-CA) to join the U.S. Senate in 2017.

CAREER AS SAN FRANCISCO DISTRICT ATTORNEY

When Kamala Harris won election as San Francisco City and county's district attorney, she became the first woman, the first African American, and first person of South Asian descent to hold that post.[1] She won the race to become California's first African American district attorney in any county, running on a platform opposing the death penalty and promising to run a more professional department that would be tougher on crime than her incumbent opponent. That's where Harris developed her widely disseminated "smart on crime" policies, which she eventually turned into a book.

Harris ran for the opportunity to take over a chaotic district attorney's office, taking an especially significant stand on enforcing domestic violence laws—promising to end pretrial diversion, which allowed serial abusers to walk free—and criticizing the low conviction rate in those cases, less than half of California's average.[2] She also criticized her predecessor for a low conviction rate in felony cases, failing to professionally manage the district attorney's office, and alienating the San Francisco Police Department.[3]

While she would be undeniably successful on the first two of those issues, the third presented one of the earliest tests of her stewardship of the department. Lastly, she opposed California's voter initiative Prop 21, which passed in 2000 and mandated pretrial detention for juvenile offenders and forced many youths age fourteen to eighteen into adult trials.[4, 5]

She won a tremendous political victory when San Francisco's Democratic Central Committee elected not to endorse the incumbent district attorney, Terence Hallinan, whose very liberal politics, penchant for fistfights, and private practice career as a defense lawyer made him an unusual choice for district attorney. Sitting on that committee were future Speaker of the House Nancy Pelosi (D-CA) and California's senior Senator Dianne Feinstein (D-CA).[6] Hallinan's luck ran out after an infamous incident where he indicted all of the top brass of the San Francisco Police Department for obstruction of justice in an incident dubbed Fajita-gate, so called after a fight where three drunk cops beat up two men and took their Mexican food.[7] The case fell apart, and Hallinan's relationship with the department would never recover.

The race was hard fought, with both of Harris's opponents highlighting her past relationship nine years earlier—drawing countercharges of sexism—with then-mayor Willie Brown, whose political career had turned sour. She also got slapped with a major fine from the San Francisco Ethics Commission, which docked her campaign $34,000 for exceeding self-imposed campaign spending limits and causing four violations just less than one month before the election.[8] It was the Ethics Commission's largest fine ever, which her campaign explained was due to confusion over changes to that law. She raised over $600,000 for the election.[9]

Before Kamala Harris won office, San Francisco prosecutors didn't even have email. "The DA's Office is a mess. It's falling apart," she told *SF Weekly* during the campaign.[10] "There's one computer for every two or three lawyers, there's no centralized database to track cases. Staff morale is low because he (Hallinan) is failing to prosecute serious and violent crimes." Among her campaign promises was protecting witnesses to crime.[11]

Harris's opponents couldn't cite any problems with her record, so they preferred to focus on her past personal relationship with Brown. It was a spectacularly unsuccessful attack, which she defused in dramatic fashion during the race in a major public forum.[12] She set up her campaign headquarters in San Francisco's Bayview–Hunters Point neighborhood, a historic African American neighborhood. It was a retail campaign, *Politico* reported:

> *"Do you guys know about campaigning with ironing boards?" she asked a group of reporters in Iowa before the midterm elections, to which no one responded that they did. "When I first ran for office, for D.A., I would grab my ironing board, I'd put it in the back seat of my car. I would then go to the local grocery store with my posters and duct tape. . . . Then I'd get out of my car, I would open the ironing board in front of the grocery store, because, you see, ironing boards were the first standing desk."*
>
> *In her later campaigns—for state attorney general and U.S. Senate—Harris would come to rely, as all California politicians do, on television advertising. But in 2003, she*

said, "I'd walk up and down the hills and knock on doors, I'd stand at bus stops starting at 6 in the morning until 8 at night, begging people to talk to me on their way to work."[13]

Harris finished second out of three candidates—ahead of Bill Fazio, a conservative candidate—in the November 2003 general election for San Francisco District Attorney, and just 2.2 percent behind Hallinan.[14] Thirty-five days later, she defeated the incumbent in a landslide and took over the department the following month.[15] Her closing argument, the final campaign mailer she sent, was a postcard with photos of all of the San Francisco DAs going back to 1900, which her campaign staff retrieved from the library. All of them were white men, and the message of the postcard read, "It's time for a change."[16]

"The greatest challenge for a district attorney," she said in her inaugural speech, "and the most serious work for us as a community, is the struggle to give meaning to justice. Let's put an end right here to the question of whether we'll be tough on crime or soft on crime. Let's be smart on crime."[17] Harris also made sure that her prosecutors had email, in addition to bringing in many of her former colleagues from Alameda County and hiring a new office manager. However, she faced a political crisis over her stance on the death penalty just three months into her term as DA.

A San Francisco police officer was murdered with an AK-47, and, three days after he was fatally shot, Harris announced that she would not seek the death penalty, angering the police union who had backed her recent campaign. The *Los Angeles Times* wrote:

Harris grimaces when asked about Espinoza's funeral service, which transformed St. Mary's Cathedral into a political theater. It happened to be her 100th day in office, and Harris sat in a front-row pew. Uniformed police officers and other mourners filled the sanctuary to overflowing. When Sen. Dianne Feinstein was introduced, it seemed likely that she would continue with her crusade against assault weapons. Instead, Feinstein called for the death penalty in this case, winning a standing ovation from police and blindsiding Harris. Later Feinstein said that if she had known that Harris opposed capital punishment, she probably wouldn't have endorsed her.

The *Times* also noted in that October 2004 article, Kamala Harris "strikes some observers as a California version of Barack Obama," for whom she had held a senatorial campaign fund-raiser before he gained national recognition after his Democratic National Convention (DNC) speech that summer had thrust him into the national spotlight. In fact, Kamala Harris also made a splash at the DNC, but it happened behind the scenes when she served on the platform committee with Chairman Terry McAuliffe. She was the guest of honor at a reception hosted by then–House Minority leader Nancy Pelosi and addressed the black caucus in a slate of speakers including then-senator Hillary Clinton (D-NY) and former senator Carol Moseley Braun (D-IL).[18]

One of her first signature initiatives as San Francisco DA was the "Back on Track" program she put in place to give first-time drug offenders an alternative to jail. She explained it in a March 2010 *Huffington Post* column just six months after the California state assembly passed a bill to expand the program statewide. Governor Arnold Schwarzenegger (R-CA) signed the bill into law:[19]

> In 2005, I created an initiative called Back On Track. It's a reentry program designed for nonviolent, first-time drug offenders. These are young people who we'd call college kids under different circumstances—mostly in their early 20's, they have no prior criminal records and were caught for low-level drug offenses. None of their cases involves gangs, guns, or weapons. But they've all arrived at the program via squad car and are facing a first felony conviction.
>
> We give them a choice: they can go through a tough, year-long program that will require them to get educated, stay employed, be responsible parents, drug test, and transition to a crime-free life, or they can go to jail. My prosecutors tell me that many defendants have heard the stories about the program and choose jail instead; jail's easier, they say. Here's why: Those who choose Back On Track plead guilty to their crime, and their sentence is deferred while they appear before a judge every two weeks for about a year. They must obtain a high-school-equivalency diploma and hold down a steady job. Fathers need to remain in good standing on their child-support payments, and everyone has to take parenting classes.

For people who hit all of these milestones, the felony charge is going to be cleared from their records.

The results speak for the wisdom of investing in reentry programs. For this population, the recidivism (or re-offense rate) is typically 50 percent or higher. Four years since the creation of this initiative, recidivism has been less than 10 percent among Back On Track graduates. And the program costs only $5,000 per person, compared to over $35,000 a year for county jail. That saves our city roughly $1 million per year in jail costs alone. When you add in the total expense of criminal prosecutions to taxpayers, including court costs, public defenders, state prison, and probation, the savings are closer to $2 million. And we cannot even begin to quantify the value of these individuals' future productivity, taxes and child support payments, or the brightened prospects for their families.[20]

Ultimately, she enrolled three hundred young people in her San Francisco "Back on Track" program with fewer than thirty re-offenders.

Harris's term of office as San Francisco's DA was not perfect. Her leadership of the office was questioned due to its loose supervision of the San Francisco PD's use of violent criminals as confidential informants, contrary to department policy, which led to a major gang-related drug dealer remaining free despite committing or ordering serious crimes, including murder and money-laundering conspiracy.[21]

An incident from that era that could surface during the 2020 primary campaign is the San Francisco DA's unconstitutional withholding of "Brady disclosures" about the woman, Deborah Madden, a drug lab technician who was convicted of domestic violence in 2008 and got caught skimming cocaine for herself out of the drugs she was testing.[22, 23] A Superior Court judge ripped the DA's office in March 2010 over the incident after prosecutors sent memos questioning Madden's results, and prosecutors ultimately dismissed six hundred cases because they continued to use her in cases. As a result, the lab was shut down. Harris told the local NBC affiliate that she only found out about the issues when they erupted into front-page news, though her top deputies were aware.[24]

Upholding a campaign promise to fight for better safety measures for the victims of crime, Harris went to Washington, DC, to testify to the House Judiciary Committee in favor of a bill creating a limited federal witness protection program for state-level crimes. Rep. Elijah Cummings (D-MA) introduced the Witness Security and Protection Act, about which Harris testified on April 24, 2007.[25] She told the committee:

> Simply put, across the country, witnesses are increasingly refusing to come forward to provide information to law enforcement or to testify in serious and gang-related criminal cases. Many witnesses simply refuse to cooperate with law enforcement and are fearful of being labeled a "snitch" or becoming victims of violence themselves. Many have received threats or have been otherwise intimidated.

This problem of witness intimidation strikes at the very heart of the American criminal justice system. Without witnesses coming forward to provide information leading to the arrest and prosecution of violent criminals, law enforcement cannot apprehend and prosecute those accused of serious and violent crimes. Indeed, the structure of our adversarial system presumes that witnesses will be available and willing to testify. The Sixth Amendment to the United States Constitution guarantees the accused the right to confront witnesses against him because it assumes that witnesses will come forward. But in an increasing number of cases, witnesses are being intimidated, threatened or even killed . . .

There is a very high level of fear of retaliation, fear which may often by driven by recent, high-profile crimes committed against witnesses who participated in witness relocation and protection programs.[26]

Kamala Harris won reelection in 2007 as San Francisco DA without any opposition, something that hadn't happened for the office in sixteen prior years.[27] It would be her last term in that office. A year later, the *New York Times* mentioned her in a May 2008 story titled, "She just might be president someday:"

Mrs. Clinton seemed to have the most success in the last months, fighting like a mama bear for her cubs. So some people look to women who have earned reputations as tough fighters: Lisa Madigan, a Democrat who is attorney general in Illinois, and mentioned as a possible successor to the embattled governor, Rod Blagojevich. On one list was Kamala Harris, an African American who is the district attorney in San Francisco.

The following year, Kamala Harris declared her candidacy for California attorney general on July 17, 2009, seeking to replace Jerry Brown, who ultimately moved from that position to governor in 2010.[28]

TAKING ON TRUANCY, AND CONTROVERSY

Three months later, Harris initiated a significant escalation in her office's anti-truancy campaign in San Francisco, which the local NBC affiliate described in their headline as, "Ambitious SF Politician Targets Truant Teens. Kamala Harris, seeking higher office, aims to curb student absences."[29] For the prior four years, her office had targeted the parents of children missing school in grades K–8. The San Francisco DA contacted 1,500 parents in those years, resulting in twenty cases against the parents of the most habitually truant kids. Her office credited the initiative with a 50 percent reduction in the truancy rate for children having more than ten absences in a school year, going down from 40 percent of students down to only 20 percent of students.

The idea behind the program was to reduce future crime by youthful offenders by ensuring more children are educated and stay in school.

Furthermore, local crime statistics showed that high-school dropouts were disproportionately the victims of violent crime themselves. The prosecutor who implemented the program recently explained its gravamen to *Vox*:

> *Katy Miller, who helped implement the program as a prosecutor under Harris, said that it's meant to use a step-by-step process of escalating intervention and consequences to push parents to get their kids to school. And the cases that get to prosecution are extreme— typically parents whose kids have missed more than 30, 60, or 80 days out of a 180-day school year. Miller had one case in court in which a child missed 178 days.*
>
> *If all of that fails, the school can refer the case to the prosecutor's office, which can threaten prosecution if there's no progress on attendance. The thinking, Miller said, is that by then a parent has already been offered help but clearly needs an extra push to take it and improve a child's attendance. And if a parent agrees to take steps to improve a child's attendance, the charges are dropped. Before the program, the prosecutor's office was, for the most part, not involved in truancy cases. But the purpose wasn't to criminalize having a truant kid, said Miller, who's now chief of alternative programs and initiatives at the San Francisco District Attorney's Office.*
>
> *"The way this model has always very intentionally been designed in every aspect of it has been to not get*

to conviction and incarceration," she told me. "It has
been to use a problem-solving court model to get people
to access the services that they need to overcome what-
ever barriers they have in their life that are keeping them
from getting their young child to school. It's not going to
be perfect. We know it's not going to be perfect, but we
want to see an improved trajectory."[30]

Miller attributed the program's success to the combined benefits of the school district's programs and the DA's forceful encouragement to students and parents to avail themselves of the help to raise their attendance.

It is important to note that a San Francisco civil grand jury report from 2003 first determined that the school district was not able to adequately enforce its attendance laws and recommended working with the DA, just months before Harris won office.[31] The grand jury's second recommendation reads, "SFUSD [the school district] should commence prompt and consistent enforcement of attendance laws, including more systematic use of truancy notices, conferences, and the appropriate cooperation with the District Attorney when necessary."[32] It even issued a follow-up report on the matter six years later in the summer of 2009, noting that schools were underreporting truancy and many of the corrective measures were only being applied late in the school year, too late to help students, and many schools were afraid of reporting because of the potential for prosecution.[33]

Her office would send out a generic anti-truancy letter to all of the parents in the school district, and a second letter to any family whose child attended a Student Attendance Review Board (SARB) hearing, which her prosecutors began attending as well. Nearly every student in the program ended the cases by simply attending school more, which was the overall goal.

"As the elected district attorney for the City and County of San Francisco, I see what happens on the back end of school failures: young lives are being lost to street violence or prison time at an appalling rate. While we must invest in effective law enforcement, we must also take seriously the task of keeping our kids in school," Harris wrote in a *San Francisco Chronicle* op-ed announcing the program on October 14, 2009, in which she told the story of a kindergartener named Michael who missed eighty days of school.[34] "Children like Michael will either get their education in the streets or in the school. The fabric of our community, and the future of our economy, depend on our ability to ensure that learning happens in the classroom." According to Harris, that student only missed three days the following school year, but only after his parents were compelled to an SARB hearing.

The following year, Kamala Harris gave a speech to a public policy forum called the California Commonwealth Club that generated national headlines after her campaign launch, where she described the program:

> *I believe a child going without education is tantamount to a crime, so I decided I was going to start prosecuting parents for truancy. Well, this was a little controversial in San Francisco [laughs] and frankly my staff went bananas, they were very concerned because we didn't know at the time whether I was going to have an opponent in my re-election race.*

But I said 'Look, I'm done. This is a serious issue, and I've got a little political capital and I'm going to spend some of it.' And this is what we did. We recognized that, in that [anti-truancy] initiative, as a prosecutor and law enforcement [official], I have a huge stick, the school district has got a carrot—let's work in tandem around our collective objective and goal, which is to get those kids in school . . .

And through that initiative we found cases like the case of the woman who was by herself, raising her three children, holding down two jobs, and homeless. She just needed some help. But by shining this infrared spotlight of "public safety" on the fact that her children aren't in school, we were able to figure that out, get her access to services that exist, and through that process, the attendance of her children improved, we dismissed the charges against her and overall we've improved attendance for this population in San Francisco by 20 percent over the last two years.[35]

Since then, progressive political thought has run in a different direction. An opinion columnist at *The Guardian* misrepresented the speech in a column slamming Harris for "laughing about jailing parents for truancy" when in reality, the program did not lock up any parents, and her laughter was focused on the idea of the popularity (or lack thereof) of her program in ultraliberal San Francisco.[36] Pulitzer Prize–winning author James Foreman, who won for his nonfiction book *Locking Up Our Own: Crime and Punishment in Black America*, decried Harris's efforts after her speech resurfaced in early 2019 when he tweeted:

> *The truancy bit remains deeply problematic. She's 100 percent right that attendance is crucial. Her error—and it is not hers alone—is believing that locking people up, or threatening to lock them up, is the way to get there. The disaster of American social policy is perfectly captured by Harris's story of the mother who she threatened with prosecution before helping with social services. That's the American way: what little help we offer poor people comes under threat of prison. But let's flip that. Offer the help straight up. Keep prosecutors out it. Poor parents don't need the threat of jail to get their kids to school. They need what the wealthy take for granted: good schools, lead-free water, safe parks, healthy food, well-stocked libraries, etc.[37]*

Of course, the entire reason Harris's office became involved in student truancy was that non-compulsory efforts to accomplish the task of bringing missing students back to school, as a last resort, and it took two grand jury reports to quantify that issue. A December 2011 report from the San Francisco Department of Children, Youth and their Families (DCYF) shows that the program was successful in reducing both habitual and chronic truancy.[38] It was an issue she would continue to champion statewide as California's attorney general, which unfortunately sometimes led to adverse results in the hands of overzealous local prosecutors, unlike the program under her administration.

SMART ON CRIME

Just a week before the truancy initiative began, Kamala Harris's book *Smart on Crime: A Career Prosecutor's Plan to Make Us Safer* was published by Chronicle Books on October 7, 2009. She coauthored the book with Joan O'C Hamilton, a former *BusinessWeek* magazine San Francisco bureau chief.

"This book is predicated on one main premise, which is that all Americans have the right to live in safe communities. Having spent nearly two decades as a courtroom prosecutor, I know that it simply is not enough to just talk tough about crime," Harris told the *Huffington Post* in an interview about the book. "I want us to be what I call 'smart on crime.' That means in order to make our communities safer, we have to take a strategic approach to changing the status quo—because our current system is failing all of us."[39]

The book's factual conclusions have withstood the test of time fairly well. It includes a lengthy first chapter on the myths surrounding crime and law enforcement, though her 2009 opinions about law enforcement and its color-blind perspective toward racial bias in policing have not.

> Crime is a non-partisan issue. Democrats, Republicans and Independents all suffer from crime. And they all want to be safe. I've never heard of a perpetrator asking to what party a victim is registered before he commits the crime . . .
>
> This book is not a comprehensive look at criminal law or criminal justice. It does not pretend to address a host of legitimate issues that law-enforcement, civil

libertarians, and victims' advocates debate, from the complexity of sentencing issues of due process and civil liberties. Rather, I want to zero in on the key opportunities I see for reform right now. They primarily involves dividing the crime problem into specific segments that we can target with more effective solutions. This includes better services to help victims are recover from the aftermath of crime. To fully understand and address those opportunities, we first need to assess the myths that have dominated the dialogue about crime and still stand in the way of doing business differently. These are the myths that lead to calcified thinking, paralysis, and a dearth of creative strategies to disrupt the cycles of crime.

On both sides of the political aisle, we urgently need a broader vision and a willingness to innovate. For the left, that means getting past biases against law-enforcement and recognizing that even lower income communities, in fact, especially low-income communities, want and deserves greater public-safety resources so that they can live free from crime. For the right, it means acknowledging that crime prevention is a key to crime fighting, and that the tools we need to ensure community safety are far more diverse than simply laws that make prison sentences longer.[40]

Later, Harris explained what she termed the "crime pyramid," which is the distribution of violent criminals versus nonviolent offenders who are caught in the criminal justice system, and how too many harsh solutions for tough offenders were applied to the "bottom" 96 percent of people charged with crimes.

However, Kamala Harris's 2009 viewpoint about law enforcement clashes with the realities about policing uncovered in America after smartphones became widespread. While she pitched her "Back on Track" initiative, Harris also supported strong enforcement of drug laws against low-level offenders. She has moved to take a new stance on criminal-justice-reform issues in the Senate, and that has won over some progressive leaders who would otherwise be the biggest critics of her vision of America in *Smart on Crime,* as *Buzzfeed News* reported:

> "Most Americans will love the fact that she was a prose-cutor," said Shaun King, a prominent criminal justice activist and the cofounder of Real Justice PAC, a group devoted to electing progressive prosecutors. "But she will have to walk a tightrope, because here's the chal-lenge with her presidential ambitions: Before you win the nomination, you have to win over the base of the party. For most of us, 'prosecutor' is not synony-mous with 'hero.'" Harris's words a decade ago about police officers in Smart on Crime, King said, made him "cringe." "She would get heckled if she said that now," he said, in an era where progressives recognize the fear and mistrust that many people of color have of law enforcement.

King, for his part, has been won over by Harris's time in the Senate, and what he calls her "evolution" on criminal justice. "I was a little slow to trust her as a reformer on criminal justice, but I think she's proven herself to me," [said King, who] disapproved of much of Harris's "moderate" work as California's attorney general. But as a senator, he said, empowered by her intimate knowledge of the justice system, "I think she's become one of the better spokespersons for really serious criminal justice reform in the Democratic Party."[41]

Her book only mentioned racial bias twice. It wouldn't be until 2016 when better statistical record keeping began to prove that police disproportionately shoot and kill African Americans.[42]

Eventually, her "smart on crime" phrase caught on nationally as an alternative to what Harris called a false choice between being tough on crime or soft on crime. When Attorney General Eric Holder created a five-point plan to maximize the Department of Justice's prosecution practices, he used the same moniker.[43]

Kamala Harris used her time at the San Francisco DA's office to create and articulate a prosecutorial philosophy that she spread nationally with the release of her book. In early 2009 she began running for California attorney general, a run that would eventually lead to national fame and a historic first term in a statewide office affecting tens of millions of people.

CALIFORNIA'S ATTORNEY GENERAL

Kamala Harris became the first California Attorney General to be a woman, the office's first African American, and its first South Asian American. But before that happened, she had to fight a six-way party primary, rose to national prominence through her ties to the White House, and survived a narrow general election.

Attorney General Harris implemented some of the programs that she began in San Francisco on a statewide basis in her role as California's top cop. She led the charge against racial bias in policing at the dawn of the Black Lives Matter movement and made a series of significant judgment calls during her six years in office before ascending to the U.S. Senate.

In March 2009, Harris got an unexpected shot in the arm when PBS's respected anchor Gwen Ifill went on the *Late Show with David Letterman* to promote her book and said this:

> *There's a great district attorney in San Francisco whose name is Kamala Harris. She's brilliant. She's smart. She doesn't look anything like anybody you see on Law and Order. She's tough. She's got a big future. People call her the female Barack Obama. . . .*[1]

Harris filed to run for attorney general a few months later. She faced the task of assembling her first statewide political candidacy and releasing her signature book, *Smart on Crime*, which was published in October of that year. The field of candidates seeking to replace Jerry Brown, who vacated the AG's office to run for governor, ballooned to six candidates, including three termed-out state assemblymen, a former Facebook official, and the former city attorney of Los Angeles.[2]

That campaign would become the first time Kamala Harris had to defend her record as San Francisco's DA, including an unintended result from her signature program, "Back on Track." As her opponents noted, the "Back on Track" program was aimed at the kinds of low-level drug dealers who often graduated to career criminals when hit with long jail sentences and punitive sentencing, but one of the participants who did reoffend happened to be an undocumented immigrant. It became a major campaign issue. Harris had to defend the unintended consequence of her program on the national stage, telling ABC News:

> *"Innovation by its very nature and definition means that you are doing something different from how it has been done before," Harris said. "And necessarily, then, there is some assumption of risk, because doing something differently than it's been done means invariably, even with the best of intentions, we'll find a glitch. There will be something that becomes obvious in hindsight that was a flaw in the design and then you fix it.*
>
> *"In that case, the Izaguirre case, that became a very obvious flaw in the design of Back on Track," Harris said.*

"I imagined many scenarios, didn't figure that one out until we realized that this was a flaw and we fixed it." Asked to identify the flaw, Harris said, "The flaw was that we hadn't imagined that there would be undocumented immigrants in the program. So we didn't set up a system for checking them."

"No one who is an undocumented immigrant should benefit from this program," Harris said. "This initiative is designed to make sure that the participant will gain legal employment and the undocumented immigrant may not obtain legal employment in our country."[3]

That wouldn't be the only time she was on the defensive about her record during the campaign. On the eve of the primary, Harris was leading the polls but fighting to defend her reputation after the crime lab technician scandal rocked her office. The technician had been convicted of domestic violence, but her top deputies didn't tell defendants and continued to use the same person to testify on behalf of their office while discussing her flaws in internal memos. Prosecutors are required to disclose any negative information about people who testify in their cases or any exculpatory information.[4] Over six hundred cases were thrown out because of the issue, and Los Angeles's NPR station, KPCC, asked Harris about the issue just a week before the primary election. She responded:

This fiasco, no doubt, highlights that there was a broken system that needed to be fixed and we're on the path to doing that. . . . As a result of this fiasco, I realized that we needed to have stricter and more concrete policies [about Brady disclosures] in my office. And so we created that. The unfortunate reality is that most DA's offices in the state, in fact, the vast majority of them do not have written policies as it relates to this issue; we were no different. But when I realized that we have someone in the police department who was convicted of a crime and we didn't know about it, it became clear that we needed to have a written policy that would have affirmative questions to the department about its personnel.[5]

She faced tough competition in the race from now-Rep. Ted Lieu (D-CA) who ran on a platform of combatting mortgage fraud and abusive practices.[6] Former Facebook security officer Chris Kelly made a YouTube video attacking Harris's record on crime, and she fired back by criticizing the social media network's complaint-provoking problems protecting its users' privacy—an ongoing problem today.[7] Another of her opponents, Alberto Torrico, was the former state assembly majority leader.[8]

Kamala Harris won a plurality in the primary with just over 33 percent of the vote on June 8, 2010, and changed her focus to Republican general election opponent Steve Cooley, the Los Angeles County DA.[9] Torrico finished second with just over 15 percent of the vote.

By then, the national media had nicknamed her the "female Obama," which is generally an electoral advantage in liberal California. Still, she was running during the Tea Party election, which energized the GOP and led to a close race. But it was more than just a nickname; it turned out that

Kamala Harris was the only "down ballot" Democrat that President Obama chose to fund-raise to support in 2010.[10]

Kamala Harris's opposition to the death penalty and Cooley's support were two of the key issues in the race. He brought up her early-career decision not to seek the death penalty for a cop killer, which even Senator Feinstein (D-CA) eventually got over and endorsed Harris in the AG race. Another key difference with Cooley's position is that Harris supported medical marijuana access back then, and the Los Angeles DA favored prosecuting dispensaries.[11] She publicly advocated for the California assembly to pass a new anti-truancy law modeled on her program in San Francisco during the campaign, and Governor Schwarzenegger signed it into law less than a month before the vote.[12]

Ten days after the election ended, Harris led Cooley by only 31,000 votes, which is a slim lead in California, a state that accepts all absentee ballots to ensure that every vote is counted.[13] Every other Democratic statewide candidate had already won their race, and she was in the last undecided race. Republican strategists considered Cooley a moderate and believed that he was close to a sure bet to win that year, but he conceded the race while trailing by 50,000 votes on Thanksgiving day 2010.[14] *Politico*'s Ben Smith, who would go on to found *Buzzfeed News*, hailed her as the "anti-Palin"[15] and the future of the Democratic Party.[16]

At first glance, the president and Harris have much in common: Both are mixed-race children of immigrants raised by a single mother; both are eloquent, telegenic big-city lawyers with strong liberal credentials who catapulted from relative obscurity to the national stage. And like the first African American president, Harris has broken a long-standing barrier—she's California's first African American attorney general and the first woman to hold the office. But Harris, whose position, potential and glamour will most likely give her as high a national profile as she wants, resists the comparisons.

"It's flattering," she told Politico, just weeks after claiming victory in a photo-finish race against Steve Cooley, her Republican opponent. Nevertheless, "these comparisons make me uncomfortable because I know what I want to do. I am really excited about being attorney general."

Harris won the race by 70,000 votes.

Her tenure as California attorney general would span six years and give arguments to both her supporters, about her progressive reforms, and her critics, who argued that she turned a blind eye to prosecutorial misconduct in California's other district attorney offices. Her anti-truancy advocacy had unintended consequences. She surprised supporters by appealing federal court rulings invalidating California's death penalty and imposing a federal monitor over its troubled prison system, which she now oversaw. Her pledge to tackle mortgage fraud didn't pan out, though she did take a major leadership role against racial bias in policing and fought to correct injustices against LGBT people, though the latter was a mixed bag.

Attorney General Harris won reelection handily in 2014, capturing a majority of votes in the state's unique "jungle primary" and finishing with 57.5 percent of the votes in the general election.[17, 18]

WINNING THE RACE

California's first female attorney general, Kamala Harris, was sworn in alongside Governor Jerry Brown by Chief Justice of California Tani Cantil-Sakauye at the California Museum for History, Women and the Arts.[19] She entered office with facing the challenge of managing one of America's most chronically overcrowded prison systems while seeking to be a reformer.

"For many offenders, prison amounts to attending crime college," the Associated Press reports Harris said about her plans to reduce incarceration for nonviolent offenders in a twenty-eight-minute speech that ran longer than that delivered by new Gov. Jerry Brown earlier in the day. "Most nonviolent offenders are learning the wrong lesson."[20] Her inaugural address also touched on the new anti-truancy law she helped pass during the campaign, which went into effect that week:

> We know chronic truancy leads to dropping out, which dramatically increases the odds that a young person will become either a perpetrator or a victim of crime. Folks, it is time to get serious about the problem of chronic truancy in California. Last year we had 600,000 truant students in our elementary schools alone, which roughly matches the number of inmates in our state prisons. Is it a coincidence? Of course not.
>
> And as unacceptable as this problem is—I know we can fix it. In San Francisco, we threatened the parents of truants with prosecution, and truancy dropped 32 percent. So, we are putting parents on notice. If you fail in

your responsibility to your kids, we are going to work to make sure you face the full force and consequences of the law. This work to combat truancy is part of the broader oath that I swore today and the oath upheld every day by the men and women of the Attorney General's office.[21]

Harris's anti-truancy program as San Francisco DA used the power of the office to bring parents to the table who wouldn't heed any other measures as a last resort, and didn't lock any of them up. But it hasn't always worked out that way, and she had no power over the way that California's new law is being applied, which disproportionately affects minorities. Orange County's recently departed district attorney, Tony Rackauckas, only used the law in the run-up to elections—which turned out to be the least of Harris's problems with him—and in one case arrested and "perp-walked" an African American mother struggling with a child afflicted with sickle-cell anemia, which caused excessive medical absences.[22] The approach that worked in San Francisco wasn't replicated throughout California.

"My regret is that I have now heard stories that in some jurisdictions DAs have criminalized the parents," she said in an April 2019 interview with *Pod Save America*, she admitted that the law had "unintended consequences" and that she would not promote the law on a national basis. "And I regret that that has happened and any thought that anything I did led to that. That was never the intention. Never the intention."

Three of her better-received initiatives as attorney general include forcing police officers to undergo antibias training aimed at reducing racial discrimination, making California's Department of Justice implement universal body cameras, and creating an innovative open-government initiative to give citizens access to law enforcement statistics. Also, Harris took steps to end the "gay panic" defense for assaults, which were ultimately successful.

Against the backdrop of a police shooting epidemic centered around Los Angeles, San Bernardino, Santa Clara, and Kern counties, Attorney General Harris launched the antibias training program in November 2015, and later expanded it.[23]

> *"In January, I began a dialogue with leaders of the California law enforcement community about strengthening the relationship of trust between law enforcement and the communities we are sworn to serve," said Attorney General Harris. "Throughout this dialogue, a theme has emerged regarding the need to continue to bring best-in-class training to law enforcement across our state. Today, we are proud to announce that the California Department of Justice is offering the first POST certified course in the nation to combine the concepts of procedural justice and implicit bias. This course is the result of a true collaboration with law enforcement, community partners and academics to bring evidence-based concepts into practice."*
>
> *The training course, titled "Principled Policing: Procedural Justice and Implicit Bias" is the result of a*

> *collaborative partnership between the California Depart-*
> *ment of Justice, the Commission on Peace Officers Stan-*
> *dards and Training, the Stockton and Oakland Police*
> *Departments, Stanford University and the California Part-*
> *nership for Safe Communities.*[24]

A year later, she created a "train the trainers" course, and her actions won the approval of two of the state's largest newspaper editorial boards.[25]

Attorney General Harris implemented a department-wide body camera program for the California DOJ in 2015. She also opened a website to increase government transparency in law enforcement, resulting in a tool anyone can (still) access at https://openjustice.doj.ca.gov/ to find out about policing in America's largest state. Her office explained the portal:

> *The Open Data Portal is an online repository of download-*
> *able criminal justice data in raw form available to the pub-*
> *lic. This tool will enable researchers, civic coders, and*
> *journalists to help tackle seemingly intractable problems in*
> *the criminal justice system. As part of the initiative, Attorney*
> *General Harris is expanding her work with law enforcement*
> *to improve reporting by eliminating unnecessary require-*
> *ments and modernizing data reporting processes.*
>
> *OpenJustice builds on Attorney General Kamala D.*
> *Harris's leadership deploying 21st century "smart on*
> *crime" approaches to improve public safety. As California's*
> *Chief Law Enforcement Officer, Attorney General Harris*

*has worked to embed new technology into the DNA of the
Department of Justice and law enforcement agencies
across the state.*[26]

Yet, when the state legislature tried to make body cameras mandatory
for all police forces, she demurred from supporting the bill, which was
opposed by law enforcement organizations—many of whom were political
supporters—and the legislation died.[27] Harris also opposed a law that
would've made California's Department of Justice the primary prosecutor
in police shootings, raising the ire of activists. She didn't support the bill
on the grounds of removing control from locally elected DAs, even though
its intent is to remove conflicts of interest between prosecutors and the
police forces they have to work with on a daily basis.[28]

Lastly, Harris led efforts to make California the first state to ban the
"gay panic" defense to murder and assaults, cosponsoring a bill in the legislature.[29] Voluntary manslaughter is a homicide committed "upon a sudden quarrel or heat of passion." The bill read:

*This bill would state that for purposes of determining
sudden quarrel or heat of passion, the provocation was
not objectively reasonable if it resulted from the discov-
ery of, knowledge about, or potential disclosure of the
victim's actual or perceived gender, gender identity, gender expression, or sexual orientation, including under
circumstances in which the victim made an unwanted
nonforcible romantic or sexual advance towards the*

defendant, or if the defendant and victim dated or had a romantic or sexual relationship.[30]

On September 27, 2014, it became law.

THE MORTGAGE FORECLOSURE CRISIS

As attorney general, Kamala Harris took on the big banks who caused America's foreclosure crisis with lax underwriting standards, and she won big. That's not to say her record was flawless, but she did get a lot more relief for her state than she could've by simply going along with what other states were doing. However, some of her record for failing to prosecute one of the industry's worst offenders will definitely become a 2020 Democratic primary campaign issue.

AG Harris pulled California out of a multistate settlement with the big banks, opting to fight for more compensation than the $2–4 billion payout that was already on the table.[31] At the time, 30 percent of households in her state were underwater—owing more on their mortgages than the value of their homes—and 7 percent were delinquent for more than ninety days and facing foreclosure. According to a report by her state attorney's office, the agreement Harris negotiated with Chase, Bank of America, and Wells Fargo and secured a minimum of $12 billion in debt relief, but ultimately reduced Californians' mortgage debts by $18 billion.[32] The other forty-nine states settled at the same time for only $25 billion, combined.

She was invited to speak to the Democratic National Convention for the first time in 2012, and delivered a short speech highlighting President Obama's support for the national mortgage foreclosure settlement.[33]

Kamala Harris also sponsored the "Homeowner Bill of Rights" which California's legislature enacted and its governor signed into law. "After the excesses and unfair practices we've seen the last two years," she wrote in an op-ed prodding the state assembly to pass her initiative.[34] "After all of the foreclosures and homes lost, I believe the evidence is in and the time is now for us to make reform real." It made a series of changes to the law aimed at ending the worst abuses in mortgage lending and servicing, with these protections for owner-occupied residences:

- No Dual-Tracking, preventing the use of foreclosure as a "stick" in the loan modification process
- Servicers Must Provide Homeowners with a Single Point of Contact
- Homeowners Have the Right to Sue for Violations
- Preforeclosure Help for Borrowers[35]

The bill additionally provided protections for tenants in homes being foreclosed, authorized statewide grand juries to expose fraud, and extended statutes of limitations on mortgage frauds in addition to giving municipalities new tools to fight foreclosure-driven blight.[36] Unfortunately, local district attorney's offices are on the front lines for enforcement of the new law, and even in large counties, most only assigned a few prosecutors to the task. At the same time, Harris opened a Mortgage Fraud Task Force, but the *East Bay Express* dubbed it "The Strike Force That Never Struck" in a long-form investigative story:

[I]nterviews and public records obtained from Harris's office reveal a portrait of a well-funded and robustly

staffed strike force that appears to have never really struck a significant blow against the foreclosure rescue scam industry in California. Instead, the job of prosecuting foreclosure consultants in the state has fallen on attorneys general from other states, private attorneys (often working pro bono), and local county district attorneys in California who have fewer resources and staff to investigate and litigate.

At the same time, foreclosure consultants have largely ignored and brazenly violated laws put in place by former Attorney General Jerry Brown that were supposed to undermine the ability of foreclosure rescue scammers to operate. California, as a result, is not only the base of operation for countless fraudsters, but also a favorite hunting ground for those who continue to prey on desperate homeowners.

A recent California Senate Banking and Financial Institutions Committee meeting included testimony from experts who reiterated that the banks that signed the National Mortgage Settlement, along with most of the other mortgage loan servicers in California, continue to break laws that were implemented to protect homeowners seeking loan modifications. Just last week, as the Express reported on its website, the California Reinvestment Coalition released a report showing that the nation's largest banks and mortgage servicing companies continue to violate standards and laws mandated by the National

Mortgage Settlement, the California Homeowner Bill of Rights, and new federal mortgage servicing rules.

"Part of the problem is that there's no enforcement of the homeowners bill of rights," said Marroquin. "When you allow the banks to continue to do what they want, people feel helpless, they look to other places for assistance, but then fall into these foreclosure rescue scams."[37]

Another high-profile case stemming from the mortgage crisis was what to do about OneWest Bank, a lender created by Goldman Sachs financier Steve Mnuchin, who went on to be the 2016 Trump campaign's national finance chair and ultimately treasury secretary. It's difficult for states to investigate federally chartered banks, and OneWest was already under a 2011 federal consent decree order with the Office of Thrift Supervision for the same illegal practices it undertook including avoiding payment of state deed taxes, robo-signing, backdating records, and abusing the state's rapid nonjudicial foreclosure process.

Kamala Harris's former deputies leaked a 2013 memo to *The Intercept* outlining their request to pursue a civil case against OneWest on the very day she was sworn in to the U.S. Senate and considering his nomination for a cabinet position.[38]

One of the supervisors involved in the OneWest case, Supervising Deputy Attorney General Benjamin Diehl, left the office in November 2013 to join Stroock & Lavan, a corporate law firm that represents Bank of America,

JPMorgan Chase, and Citigroup in cases against con-
sumers, regulatory agencies and state attorneys general.
Emails indicate that Diehl arranged private meetings with
Stroock partners six months before his hiring, while he
still worked for the attorney general. Stroock would not
make Diehl available for comment.

Harris's prodigious fund-raising also raises questions
about how attentive she is to the needs of campaign con-
tributors. Prior to signing on with Trump, Mnuchin donated
to members of both parties. He gave $2,000 to Harris's
Senate campaign in February 2016. Among the investors
in OneWest Bank was major Democratic donor George
Soros, who maxed out to Harris's campaign in 2015.

While the OneWest memo's cover page read "Case NOT filed despite strong recommendations," the memo only termed the overall likelihood of success as "moderate" and noted that it would be a novel case of first impression. That means her own team rated it as one of the most difficult kind of cases to win in court, since there's no precedent to guide the judge or jury, and noted it was likely to be resource intensive, as well as to result in an extensive appellate process lasting three to five years, with the chance that a judge might not award significant relief for their efforts. "We went and we followed the facts and the evidence, and it's a decision my office made," she told *The Hill* in response. "We pursued it just like any other case. We go and we take a case wherever the facts lead us."[39] Senator Harris voted against Mnuchin's confirmation as treasury secretary.

CHILDREN'S ADVOCACY

In early 2015, Attorney General Harris created the California Children's Bureau of Justice (CBJ). One of its first initiatives was combating identity theft among foster kids, and using the department's data to find child abuse cases that might've slipped through the cracks in the system.[40] "When I created the Bureau of Children's Justice, I did it for one reason: We can't let down our most vulnerable today, and then lock them up tomorrow," Harris wrote on Facebook announcing the new department.[41] After a series of discussions with stakeholders, the CBJ identified five main areas to focus upon:

- California's foster care, adoption, and juvenile justice systems
- Discrimination and inequities in education
- California's elementary school truancy crisis
- Human trafficking of vulnerable youth
- Childhood trauma and exposure to violence[42]

A year later, the BCJ announced five different investigations of different child welfare issues. Three targeted counties, one targeted a school district, and the other went after a private school operator.[43]

One of those investigations reached settlement in 2018, when Humboldt County admitted that it was seriously delinquent in reporting child abuse. The county agreed to institute a 24/7 response system and promised to switch to electronic reporting of child abuse cases.[44]

Another investigation into the Stockton County Unified School District's policing practices led to 34,000 criminal arrests from 1991 to 2019 in a school district that typically serves 39,000 students annually.

For perspective, that means that over twelve hundred arrests annually touched 2.5 kids out of every hundred students in the district who were arrested by police. Sixteen hundred of those arrests were of children under the age of 10.

The BCJ obtained a twenty-six-page court order in February 2019, which *Yes!* Magazine described as "more like a detailed school policy document rather than a general court order—a blueprint for other districts that suffer from over policing."[45]

> *"They called the cops on my [first-grader] son" three times for playing too long at recess, Glenda Sanchez, one of the parents who protested school policies, told KXTV-TV in Sacramento.*
>
> *In one case, a 5-year-old boy was handcuffed and arrested after he lashed out at a school officer during a meeting at school. The boy had a diagnosis with attention deficit hyperactivity disorder, and the story was picked up by news outlets around the world.[46]*

Shockingly, Stockton's policing problem began when they hired more security after a horrifying 1989 school shooting in San Diego led to the state's first assault weapons ban. Stockton's school police conducted a thousand arrests in its first year alone. But now the district's staff will undergo training in the Constitution, the Civil Rights Act, and the Americans with Disabilities Act, all because Kamala Harris recognized that there was a systemic issue.

CONTROVERSIAL HANDLING OF PROSECUTORIAL MISCONDUCT AND WRONGFUL CONVICTION CASES

It is fair to say that Kamala Harris's record handling prosecutorial misconduct cases as attorney general was either tough on bad DAs or smart on bad DAs. The *New York Times* covered two terrifying high-profile cases in 2016, where California DAs were caught doing the unthinkable and hiding behind prosecutorial immunity:

> In 2015, judges called out her office for defending convictions obtained by local prosecutors who inserted a false confession into the transcript of a police interrogation, lied under oath and withheld crucial evidence from the defense. "Talk to the attorney general and make sure she understands the gravity of the situation," federal appellate Judge Alex Kozinski instructed one of Harris's deputies in court last year. Harris says that as a career prosecutor, she takes allegations of misconduct very seriously. "My office evaluates each case based on the facts and the evidence," she told me.

The prosecutor in that case received a slap on the wrist, just a one-year suspension from the practice of law.[47] The *Times* continued:

> Harris has also been criticized for her response to accusations of misconduct by prosecutors and sheriff's deputies in Orange County. Two years ago, Scott Sanders,

an assistant public defender in Orange County, discovered hidden records showing that sheriff's deputies in the local jails were placing coveted informants in cells next to inmates who were awaiting trial—and for decades maintaining a secret database about them. *(author's emphasis) The district attorney's office also appears to have repeatedly failed to disclose evidence from its own files on some informants. Defendants were convicted based on the testimony of informants whose credibility, the secret records showed, prosecutors and the police questioned, unknown to the judge and jury. One informant labeled "unreliable" helped convict a man who was executed in 1998 for a murder he insisted he did not commit. Last March, following the revelations about the database, a judge described the performance of the Orange County district attorney's office, in the murder case before him, as "sadly deficient" and instructed Harris and her office to take over the case.*[48]

Instead of acting against the longtime Orange County District Attorney Tony Rackauckas, the attorney general defended him by appealing the order that her office take over the tainted case at hand.[49] Her office argued that the blame rested instead with the Orange County Sheriff's Office, but judges flatly rejected that argument, noting that the only reason for cops to create a well-organized stable of jailhouse informants was to benefit prosecutors who used their lies to obtain convictions. Rackauckas was voted out of office in November 2018.[50]

Harris admitted to the *Times* that she knew about the Orange County Jailhouse informant scandal, which sunk at least twenty felony cases, some of them for murder. A panel of judges did not pull punches describing the scheme:

> *The magnitude of the systemic problems cannot be overlooked. The record before us demonstrates that from the outset, the Orange County district attorney's office (OCDA) failed in its duty as the primary county prosecutor to supervise its prosecution team, specifically the Orange County Sheriff's Department (OCSD), and ensure its prosecutors and its law enforcement team complied with its constitutional and statutory obligations.*[51]

There is another case tried by the attorney general's office during Harris's tenure which has infuriated activists, involving a wrongfully convicted seventy-seven-year-old man. George Gage had no criminal history, but was convicted of sex crimes on the word of only his accuser at a second trial after a 1998 complaint from his stepdaughter. The judge in that case requested and obtained exculpatory evidence from prosecutors—which should've by law been turned over *before* the trial—and set aside Gage's conviction. But the prosecutors in that case successfully appealed the loss and got that judge removed from the bench, reassigning the case to another jurist, who issued the wrongfully convicted man a *seventy-year* sentence.

By the time Attorney General Harris's office was working on the case, many years had passed, and her deputy noted to the court that they could uphold Gage's conviction on a technicality, even though the evidence was completely exonerating, and had been in prosecutors' hands for twenty years. The judges did so, and Gage is still in jail.[52]

OTHER CASES

Attorney General Harris was an early supporter of using DNA searches to solve previously unsolvable crimes.[53] She told the *Los Angeles Times* why in 2011, "California is on the cutting edge of this in many ways. I think we are going to be a model for the country. I really do." In 2018, the technique famously solved a thirty-year-old cold-case mystery to bring the Golden State Killer to justice.[54] However, it is still considered a controversial use of technology to solve crimes.

She also led the charge against backpage.com, which ultimately led the classified ads website to shut down. It was one of her final major acts as California AG. After arresting backpage's CEO Carl Ferrer, she lobbied to change federal law to remove protections from internet websites and publishers who provide dating services, which have been illegally used by some to promote prostitution or escort services.[55] Ferrer later pled guilty to money laundering and conspiracy to facilitate prostitution charges and cooperated with authorities against the site's founders.[56] Her opponents consider her support for those changes to the law as linked to her relationship with the music (RIAA) and recording industry's (MPAA) lobbying arms, and as a form of subtle censorship as well as raising barriers of entry to small business.[57]

"As attorney general of California, I have vigorously defended the constitutionality of the Affordable Care Act (ACA)," wrote Harris in a 2015 *Huffington Post* column titled "Protecting Health Care for All" explaining why California filed a brief in support of the ACA the landmark case *King v. Burwell* in the Supreme Court.[58] "This landmark law has brought much-needed reform and accountability to our health care system. And despite what you may have heard, it's changed millions of lives for the better." Ultimately, the Supreme Court upheld the ACA.

When an oil pipeline on the California coast burst, Harris personally intervened in the case, which resulted in four felony charges and forty-two other criminal counts.[59] She also initiated a major price-fixing investigation against California's largest oil companies after consumers in her state paid premiums of fifty cents to a dollar per gallon on gasoline.[60]

After U.S. Attorney General Eric Holder sharply curtailed the use of civil asset forfeiture, the process by which federal law enforcement can seize property used in or acquired through crimes even without a conviction, Harris cosponsored a bill that would've delegated those powers to California law enforcement.[61] Had it passed, it would've allowed state cops to seize property merely if they considered filing criminal charges.

One of Harris's deputies caused a stir in a 2014 oral argument, when he argued in federal court that the state opposed programs that would get more inmates out of jail because their labor was needed to fight fires, which she was shocked to learn from the news, and disparaged as "evoking chain gangs."[62] California does rely on about 4,400 prisoners to assist in firefighting, who represent just over 2.6 percent of the overall prison population and are paid $2 a day, but the court didn't buy the argument and ordered more people released from the state's overcrowded prisons.[63] The state's prison system is notoriously overcrowded, partly thanks to the "Three Strikes" law that imposes harsh mandatory minimums sentences on repeat offenders.

During her attorney general campaign, Harris penned an op-ed opposing Arizona's 2010 law that effectively criminalized being an undocumented immigrant and told state law enforcement to police the federal issue of proper residency.[64] Once in office, she continued to advocate for undocumented immigrants, filing a 2012 brief in support of Sergio Garcia, a "Dreamer" who was brought to the United States as a baby and passed the California bar, but was denied admission over his immigration status.[65] It took two more years for the case to be heard, and eventually for legislation to be passed, but Garcia did get his bar card, and in 2015 he earned a green card allowing him to both work *and* practice law in California.[66]

HARRIS'S RUN FOR THE SENATE

Kamala Harris declared her candidacy for the U.S. Senate on January 13, 2015, becoming the first person in the race to replace retiring Senator Barbara Boxer (D-CA). Right off the bat, the Democratic Senatorial Campaign Committee (DSCC) openly supported her candidacy.[67] The national political action committee Emily's List also signaled its support early in the campaign.

Ten-term U.S. Rep. Loretta Sanchez (D-CA) emerged fairly early as Harris's top competition for the Senate seat. Thirty-six other candidates would follow and run in the primary election.[68] On day one of the campaign, Senator Elizabeth Warren (D-MA) endorsed her, and Senators Cory Booker (D-NJ) and Kirsten Gillibrand (D-NY) both celebrated her entry into the race:

On Tuesday evening, New Jersey Sen. Cory Booker tweeted that he was "So Excited about @KamalaHarris campaign for California US Senate seat," encouraging his followers to visit her website. New York Sen. Kirsten Gillibrand also offered some words of praise, tweeting that she was, "Excited to see @KamalaHarris announce she's running." Gillibrand also retweeted a tweet from Harris linking to her campaign website.[69]

All of them are now her 2020 Democratic primary opponents. She also won an endorsement from California's popular Governor Brown during the primary.[70]

Harris raised almost $6 million in 2015 and nearly $10 million just for the primary race, but early on, her spending on lavish hotels and first-class plane tickets attracted unwanted attention.[71] But the issue didn't faze voters, nor members of the California Democratic Party, who gave her 78 percent of the convention vote to endorse her candidacy, which meant that the party only spent money supporting Harris even though it was a race with two Democrats.[72, 73]

Harris won a strong plurality in the thirty-seven-way primary with over 37 percent of the vote, and Rep. Sanchez only captured just over 17 percent of ballots cast, which meant that it would be an all-Democratic general election for California's senate seat.[74]

The biggest endorsement came in the general election from Barack Obama, the president of the United States, and his vice president, Joe Biden, who is also running for the 2020 Democratic presidential nomination.[75] Harris's opponent Rep. Sanchez complained bitterly about the president's endorsement, but it's no surprised that Obama would endorse Harris, considering that Harris began supporting him in 2004, before he even hit the national spotlight.[76] Even during the race, there was open speculation that President Obama might seek to nominate her to the Supreme Court.[77]

Rep. Sanchez made national headlines for doing the "dab" on stage during a televised debate, making the attorney general laugh and declare, "So, there's a clear difference between the candidates in this race."[78] The Harris campaign spokesman mocked Sanchez, saying, "Her dab was as weak as the rest of her debate performance." In the end, Harris raised $15 million for the race and carried a major lead in the polls throughout the general election.

At age fifty-two, Kamala Harris won her senate race by a blowout margin of 61.6 percent of the vote to Rep. Sanchez's 38.4 percent of ballots cast.[79] She became just the second African American woman to serve in the United States Senate, and the first woman of South Asian descent as well.

Senator-elect Harris addressed a crowd of her supporters the night of the 2016 election after her race was decided, but grim results loomed in the presidential election. Harris delivered a stirring call to action:

> *I believe this is that moment in time that many of us in our personal lives have faced, when we had to look in a mirror because of circumstances in a situation we had to look in a mirror and with furrowed brow we asked a question: Who are we?*
>
> *I believe this is that moment in time for our country where we are collectively being required to look in a mirror and with furrowed brow we are asking a question: Who are we in California? I believe the answer is a good one. We are*

a great country . . . And part of what makes us great is fighting for our ideals, fighting to make sure those words always ring true that we spoke in 1776 that we are all, and should be treated as equals. Let's fight for our ideals and this is a moment that is challenging us, and I know we will rise to the occasion. I know we will rise to the occasion.

So let's remember what Coretta Scott King told us so long ago. She famously said, "the fight for civil rights, the fight for justice, the fight for equality, must be fought and won . . . with each generation." She had two points. It is the very nature of this fight for civil rights and justice and equality that whatever gains we make they will not be permanent, so we must be vigilant. The second point then is this, understanding that, do not despair, do not be overwhelmed, do not throw up our hands when it is time to roll up our sleeves and fight for who we are. And that's what we are about to do, and I could not be more proud to represent my beautiful state.[80]

Kamala Harris would go to Washington, DC, the following year, when she would leverage her legal experience and prosecutorial mind-set into a national leadership role that exceeds that of the typical freshman senator.

SENATE CAREER

S enator Kamala Harris was sworn in on January 3, 2017, by then–Vice President Joe Biden with her husband Doug standing by her side.[1] She was immediately joined by her stepchildren, her sister Maya, her brother-in-law Tony West (who was still an Obama DOJ official at the time), and two dozen other members of her immediate and extended family from as far away as Canada and India. "She's the best," said Biden, who is now her top opponent for the 2020 Democratic nomination, adding for emphasis, "She's the very best."

The Harris family smiles at that ceremonial swearing-in ceremony belied the senator's and the nation's concerns about the incoming Trump administration. Senator Harris's short career in Washington, DC, has in many ways has been defined by resistance to the president.

Senator Harris's top accomplishments in Congress have centered around her tough questions in committee hearings. The only reason those moments happened is that Democratic leadership placed her immediately onto some of the most desirable panels as a freshman member, including the Senate Committee for the Judiciary, the Senate Select Committee on Intelligence, the Senate Committee on the Budget, and the Senate Committee on Homeland Security and Government Affairs (HSGAC). Her highest-profile moments in committees are detailed in Chapter 3 of this book.

She and Sen. Cory Booker (D-NJ) became only the second and third African American members of the Senate Judiciary Committee in its 203-year history.[2]

HARRIS'S BILLS

Senator Harris introduced forty-five bills and six resolutions in her first term in Congress. Three of her bills became law, and three of her resolutions were passed by the Senate. A fourth bill she introduced in the 116th Congress became law in January 2019.

Senator Harris's first item to pass was a Senate resolution condemning hate crime and any other form of racism, religious, or ethnic bias, discrimination, incitement to violence, or animus targeting a minority in the United States.[3] It was cosponsored by two Democratic senators and two Republican senators.

Two bills Senator Harris wrote to assist those afflicted by natural disasters and to assess fatalities after those disasters both became law. The COUNT Victims Act was submitted on June 7, 2018, attached to a larger bill and became law as part of the FAA Reauthorization Act on October 5, 2018.[4] In the wake of a Harvard study, the bill mandated that the Federal Emergency Management Agency (FEMA) establish a formal study to create a uniform method for counting fatalities after a disaster. A study published in the *New England Journal of Medicine* by the T.H. Chan School of Public Health and other independent researchers found that victims of Hurricane Maria were grossly undercounted, believing that four thousand people died from the storm, but less than a hundred were initially reported by Puerto Rico's government.[5] In December 2017, government officials reported sixty-four storm fatalities, but in August 2018 they revised their figure up to 2,975.[6]

Five days later, Senator Harris's introduced the Disaster Victims Passport and ID Relief Act of 2018, which waived fees for government document replacements for disaster victims, and designated childcare services as "critical," thereby allowing emergency funding to assist parents who are victims of natural disasters.[7] That bill also got incorporated into the FAA Reauthorization Act and passed into law.

She introduced the Justice for Victims of Lynching Act at the end of June 2018, and it passed the Senate in December 2018 with a voice vote, but didn't become law.[8] The purpose of the bill is to specify that lynching is a civil rights crime punishable by up to ten years in prison. Senator Harris reintroduced the Act in February 2019, and again passed it in the Senate with a voice vote, where it awaits passage in the House of Representatives as of April 22, 2019.[9] As discussed in Chapter 4, the senator's bill to send more funds to historically black colleges and universities passed into law in March 2019 as part of a larger measure,

Senator Harris cosponsored a high-profile bill to reform America's cash-bail system with Senator Rand Paul (R-KY) titled the Pretrial Integrity and Safety Act.[10]

The senator also sponsored a bill to add forty-four acres to historic John Muir Park just outside San Francisco, which passed, in addition to a bill adding a marker recognizing the 1928 Saint Francis Dam disaster outside of Los Angeles, which led to California adopting new licensing standards for civil engineering.[11, 12]

OTHER HEARINGS

Senator Harris has a vast reservoir of skill at testing the mettle of presidential appointees. In addition to the highest-profile hearings discussed in Chapter 3 of this book, she had numerous other strong performances as an interrogator including questioning:

- Central Intelligence Agency (CIA) Director nominee Gina Haspel during her confirmation hearings
- Facebook COO Sheryl Sandberg
- Former Department of Homeland Security (DHS) Secretary Kirstjen Nielsen

Senator Harris sits on the Senate Intelligence Committee, which receives top secret briefings, and from the first month of her assignment there has been investigating 2016 Russian election interference. Then–CIA Deputy Director Gina Haspel was already Senate-confirmed for her position when she attended a confirmation hearing in May 2017. However, she had never been publicly asked about her time in a "black site" during the early 2000s when the Bush administration wrote memos authorizing torture of prisoners.

It was a major government scandal when revealed, because America violated its treaty obligations against torture. It was a major political issue during those hearings because President Trump openly advocated for the torture of prisoners. In a sharp, five-minute exchange, Harris got Haspel to openly break with Trump on the issue of torture, putting her on the record against illegal and barbarous practices toward U.S. captives.

"The President has asserted that torture works. Do you agree with that statement?" asked Harris.[13] "Senator, I don't believe that torture works," replied Haspel, who became the first female CIA director, but without Harris's vote.[14]

Senator Harris's revelatory questioning of Facebook COO Cheryl Sandberg grabbed headlines in September 2018, after the tech executive's answers were wishy-washy and inconclusive, like her boss's replies to the committee. "I asked Facebook CEO Mark Zuckerberg on April 10, 2018, and he said, 'The Internet Research Agency, the Russian firm ran about $100,000 worth of ads.' Following the hearing, I asked Facebook the same question in writing and on June 8, 2018," said Harris after the hearing ended. "We received a response that said, 'We believe the annual revenue that is attributable to inauthentic or false accounts is immaterial.' So my question is what did you mean by immaterial?" Sandberg was unable to clarify the exact amount that Facebook profited from Russian propaganda campaigns in the 2016 presidential election. "Any amount is too much," wrote the senator's office about the hearing.[15]

Harris convinced the social media executive to apologize for her company's policies, which contained unacceptable tolerance for white nationalism and hatred, in a rapid-fire exchange at the hearing.

> HARRIS: So my concern is that, according to Facebook's community standards, you do not allow hate speech on Facebook, however contrary to what we have seen, on June 28, 2017, a ProPublica report found that Facebook's training materials instructed reviewers to delete hate

speech targeting white men but not against Black children because Black children are not a protected class. Do you know anything about that and can you talk to me about that?

SANDBERG: I do, and what that was I think a bad policy that's been changed, but it wasn't saying that Black children, it was saying that children, it was saying that different groups weren't looked at the same way and we fixed it.[16]

The border state senator has used her office to be a fierce advocate for immigrants, and in her role on the Senate HSGAC[17] Committee she has intensely questioned former Department of Homeland Security Secretary Kirstjen Nielsen about her policy to lock kids in cages and separate families.

Senator Harris pinned Nielsen down on the question of her office having a policy of separating families seeking asylum along America's southern border. "We do not have a policy to separate children from their parents," Secretary Nielsen said to Harris in May 2018, lying about the department's policy that the senator said is causing "irreparable harm." "Our policy is, if you break the law we will prosecute you. You have an option to go to a port of entry and not illegally cross into our country."

"I'm calling on Kirstjen Nielsen to resign as Secretary of Homeland Security," the senator tweeted a month later.[18] "Under her watch, our government has committed human rights abuses by breaking up families along the southern border. And she has failed to be accountable to and transparent with the American people." CNN reports:

The Trump administration's zero-tolerance policy at the border has resulted in thousands of family separations. The policy hasn't deterred immigrants from trying to enter the country illegally, internal Department of Homeland Security documents obtained by CNN show Monday.

Harris has previously criticized the separation of undocumented children from their parents, calling it "human rights abuse"—and has frequently and famously butted heads with Nielsen and her predecessor John Kelly. But Monday's statement marks the first time the Democratic senator has called for the DHS secretary's resignation, her office confirmed to CNN. The administration's "zero-tolerance" policy has sparked a backlash from Democrats and condemnation from some Republicans as well, including former first lady Laura Bush, who called it "cruel" and "immoral" in a Washington Post *op-ed.*[19]

Harris's office even posted a petition for her constituents to sign demanding Nielsen's resignation from atop the department.[20] Then in October 2018, Harris extracted what can only be termed an Orwellian response from Nielsen at another HSGAC hearing about President Trump's policy of locking kids in cages, which she denied, but was actually happening.

HARRIS: The [Inspector General (I.G.) report indicates [that Customs and Border Patrol] (CBP) . . . has detained children and not only has CBP detained children, they've detained them for longer than is statutorily allowed. How do you reconcile the I.G. report with your testimony?

NIELSEN: We do not detain children. What we do is when we apprehend them at a border patrol station, we process them and as soon as there is room in an HHS facility we transfer them. Because of the vast . . .

HARRIS: So does the processing involve detention?

NIELSEN: We—it's not a detention facility.

HARRIS: Do they stay in CBP custody; do they spend the night there?

NIELSEN: We are not able to under the law put them anywhere else. So we will care for them until bed space opens at a detention facility at HHS.

HARRIS: In other words, you do detain children.[21]

"Tonight, in a bombshell NBC News report, I revealed a previously secret document that shows the Trump administration deliberately plotting to create a crisis at the southern border," wrote Senator Jeff Merkley (D-OR) in January 2019.[22] "The memo, dated December 2017, details deliberate plans to implement a family separation policy as a deterrent to would-be asylum seekers and lays out strategies to increase detention of migrant children. Tonight's newly-exposed document explicitly reveals that high-level administration officials lied at key points about how and why the Trump administration created this crisis."[23]

Senator Harris has used a combination of her post on the committee overseeing the Department of Homeland Security, introducing new legislation that was outlined in Chapter 4, and collaboration with other senators. That's how Kamala Harris has advanced her policy of leading the resistance to President Trump's hard-line policies on immigration.

LEGISLATIVE IDEOLOGY

An independent analysis of the bills that Senator Harris sponsored and cosponsored from 2017 through 2019 by the independent political website GovTrack.us rates her as the fourth most liberal member of the Senate.[24] In comparison, her opponents in the 2020 Democratic primary include Sen. Amy Klobuchar (D-MN), who is rated the thirty-fourth most liberal senator, then Sen. Cory Booker (D-NJ) is ranked seventeenth most liberal, Sen. Elizabeth Warren (D-MA) is ranked thirteenth most liberal, and Sen. Sanders is ranked second most liberal, while Sen. Kirsten Gillibrand (D-NY) is ranked the most liberal member of the Senate.

GovTrack's proprietary leadership rankings based upon how many bills she sponsored or cosponsored ranked her as submitting fifty-two bills in in the 115th Congress from 2017 to 2019, which the twentieth most bills submitted in the entire Senate and second most among freshman senators. Harris cosponsored 396 bills, which indicates that she's willing to work collaboratively with others to achieve her goals. Their scorecard also reveals that eight of those bills had a cosponsor in committee leadership who would oversee the bill and she only had fourteen GOP cosponsors on her fifty-two submitted bills. Three of her bills became law in the 115th Congress.

Senator Harris's bills had significant sponsorship in the House, with thirteen of her bills sponsored in the lower chamber, the most of any freshman senator. Eight of her bills in the 115th Congress got voted out of committee, three of them were resolutions which passed, three became law, a fourth became law under a House companion bill, and one died without getting a floor vote.

Senator Harris missed only two of the 599 votes in the 115th Congress, which is 0.3 percent of the total over the its two-year term. In contrast to her opponents, Sen. Warren didn't miss any votes during that two-year period, Sen. Sanders missed fifteen votes, Sen. Klobuchar missed three votes. Sen. Booker missed 4.7 percent of the total votes, twenty-eight in all, over the same two-year span.

PRE-CAMPAIGN STATEMENTS

Early in Senator Harris's term, she launched new legislation to ensure the right to counsel for undocumented immigrants, blossoming into the "anti-Sessions" as *Vox* later called her when she pledged to withhold a key vote unless Dreamers are protected.[25] It's no surprise, as Harris began those efforts while California's state attorney general and she is the first-generation American daughter of two immigrants.[26]

Dreamers are recipients of a special immigration program started by President Obama to protect nearly a million children of undocumented immigrants who have grown up in America, have clean records, but aren't citizens of the United States. In early 2018, she supported a bipartisan proposal to give Dreamers a pathway to citizenship.[27]

At the end of 2017, Senator Harris publicly called for the president's resignation over sexual assault allegations.[28] Three accusers stepped forward and asked Congress to investigate their claims of sexual impropriety against Trump. That's when Harris told *Politico*'s David Siders that Trump should quit "in the best interests of the country."[29]

Senator Harris didn't announce her presidential run until January 2019, but her pre-campaign began with national stops during the 2018 midterm elections. That's when an unusual situation unfolded on Fox News in mid-October 2018, just ten days after Senator Harris's high-profile role in the Kavanaugh hearings. The network displayed the former prosecutor's image on-screen while talking about a suspected murderer and sex offender. A Fox anchor apologized publicly to Harris.[30] In early December, Larry Wallace, her longtime staffer and senior adviser in the senator's Sacramento office, resigned in disgrace after a sexual harassment settlement from his time as Harris's high-ranking deputy at the California DOJ emerged in the *Sacramento Bee*.[31] Senator Harris is active in the #MeToo movement and has submitted a bill banning nondisclosure agreements in workplace sexual-harassment lawsuits.

Early in her presidential run, Senator Harris released ten years' worth of tax returns revealing $157,000 in annual income from her job in Congress and $320,000 in book royalties during the most recent year provided.[32]

ANALYSIS: HARRIS'S CHANCES FOR WINNING THE NOMINATION AND PRESIDENCY

amala Harris launched her 2020 Democratic primary campaign with a surge of support and a twenty-thousand-person person rally in Oakland, California.[1] She has remained a steady top three in early polling since then, trailing Senator Bernie Sanders in his second run and former Vice President Joe Biden.[2] The California senator is an early front-runner, leading the fund-raising race for large donors with $12 million raised, 98 percent of it raised from 219,000 small donors, and $9 million on hand at the end of the first quarter of 2019.[3–5] "No corporate PACs. No federal lobbyists. A real, grassroots campaign," she tweeted, "by the people and for the people."[6]

Harris is staking her campaign on her stage presence, her evenhanded prosecutorial demeanor, and her adroit rhetoric. She could take advantage of the Democratic primary's proportional representation system, which only gives delegates to candidates who win more than 15 percent of the vote, if she wins big in her home state of California.[7]

Senator Harris has not taken the time to flesh out many of her major policy priorities with legislation or a complete foreign policy platform. The Kamala Harris For The People website does not have a section on policy. She is a cosponsor of Senator Bernie Sanders's signature "Medicare for All" initiative and supports the Green New Deal proposed by Rep. Alexandria Ocasio-Cortez (D-NY) as a starting point for the discussion about combating global climate change. Recent polling from the nonprofit Kaiser Family Foundation finds that public support is very high to treat health care as a right, and she believes that private insurance plans should be limited to supplemental coverage.[8]

"Kamala Harris is definitely a charismatic figure. Definitely someone who can command an audience, definitely one who can hold her own," says SiriusXM radio host Rev. Matsimela Mapfumo (Mark Thompson), who has covered Kamala Harris's political career on his long-running morning show *Making It Plain* since the 2016 election, and who has personally interviewed her numerous times.[9] "There's a lot of substance there in terms of her as a woman, a politician, a candidate. She's not disappointing."

"I am so proud to be a daughter of Oakland, California. And as most of you know, I was born just up the road at Kaiser Hospital. And it was just a few miles away my parents first met as graduate students at UC Berkeley, where they were active in the civil rights movement," Harris said at her massive campaign kickoff rally.[10] "They were born half a world apart from each other. My father, Donald, came from Jamaica to study economics. My mother, Shyamala, came from India to study the science of fighting disease. They came here in pursuit of more than just knowledge. Like so many others, they came in pursuit of a dream." She continued:

And that dream was a dream for themselves, for me and for my sister Maya. As children growing up here in the East Bay, we were raised by a community with a deep belief in the promise of our country—and, a deep understanding of the parts of that promise that still remain unfulfilled. We were raised in a community where we were taught to see a world, beyond just ourselves. To be conscious and compassionate about the struggles of all people. We were raised to believe public service is a noble cause and the fight for justice is everyone's responsibility. In fact, my mother used to say "don't sit around and complain about things, do something."

Basically I think she was saying. You've got to get up and stand up and don't give up the fight! And it is this deep-rooted belief that inspired me to become a lawyer and a prosecutor. It was just a couple blocks from this very spot that nearly thirty years ago as a young district attorney I walked into the courtroom for the very first time and said the five words that would guide my life's work: "Kamala Harris, For the People."

"I think she was already on her way to really where she was headed, an opportunity for success, but I think the Kavanaugh hearings really set her apart," says Thompson, who noted that Harris will face questions about her past work in district attorney's offices and as California's attorney general. "There are those, obviously, who have some concern about her career as a prosecutor, but I think that experience served her well in the Kavanaugh hearings."

In late April 2019, she is placing third in five out of the six major national polls—excepting fourth place behind Representative Beto O'Rourke in the Quinnipiac poll—which are tracked by *Real Clear Politics*, running only behind Biden and Sanders.[11]

However, Harris is only running in fifth place in polls of the early primary state of New Hampshire, which she visited in mid-February for the first time, while South Bend Mayor Pete Buttigieg has soared to third place in recent surveys.[12, 13] Still, in early April 2019, CNN reported that only one out of every twenty voters is decided at this early stage in the race.[14]

She is running fourth in the major Iowa polls behind Biden, Sanders, and Buttigieg after the latter's political star took off after a CNN town hall.[15]

Harris polled third in a February 2019 Emerson University poll of another crucial early primary state, South Carolina.[16] A poll of South Carolina by Change Research in April 2019 placed Harris in third with 10 percent, with former Georgia House Minority leader Stacy Abrams in fourth with 7 percent support, though at the time of this writing it's not expected that she will join the race.[17] She didn't exceed the 1 percent mark in a poll by the Institute of Politics of voters aged eighteen to twenty-nine that named Senator Bernie Sanders as the highest rated candidate.[18]

Early Wisconsin polling in March 2019 showed Senator Sanders was the clear leader and Harris placed fifth with 5 percent of the vote, but that primary contest is relatively late in the 2020 primary season and a lot has happened since that poll.[19] A poll conducted in Florida by Bendixen &

Amandi showed that Senator Harris is in third place with 9 percent support as of March 2019, but trailing Biden by seventeen points and Sanders by just 2 percent.

Conventional wisdom is that Kamala Harris will have to make a tremendous showing in California in 2020 if she wants to win the Democratic nomination, as well as winning a significant share of South Carolina's early primary and in other large states that are rich in her target Democratic voters.

Senator Harris has picked up a significant batch of early endorsements in both her home state of California and in the early primary state of South Carolina. Early on, three quarters of the state's Democratic caucus endorsed her, including numerous state legislators, along with three U.S. Representatives, including her former opponent for attorney general and leader of the Resistance Rep. Ted Lieu.[20] She completed what amounts to a clean sweep of endorsements from statewide elected Democrats in California by the end of February, including its new Governor Gavin Newsom, who got elected as mayor of San Francisco in the same election she won as its district attorney.[21]

"I'm very enthusiastic about Kamala Harris," [Governor] Newsom said in an interview with MSNBC's Chris Hayes. "I've known her for decades, not only as district attorney where she did an extraordinary job with a very progressive record, but I watched her up close as lieutenant governor, when she served as attorney general, and I have the privilege of working with her as a U.S. senator. I think the American people could not do better."[22]

Senator Harris's diverse endorsements in South Carolina include some of the state's highest-ranking African American politicians, including the influential I. S. Leevy, one of the first black lawmakers elected since reconstruction, and others:[23]

Harris's campaign told the Associated Press that she is being endorsed by a trio of black legislators: state Reps. Pat Henegan and J. A. Moore and state Sen. Darrell Jackson. Also backing her campaign are former gubernatorial candidate Marguerite Willis and Berkeley County Democratic Chairwoman Melissa Watson.[24]

"As a result of our rapport, she actually asked, before I could ask her to come visit me, because I had planned to see her on the campaign trail, but on April 5, 2019, she asked if she could come see me in my SiriusXM studio, and that's exactly what she did," says Thompson, who spoke with the senator live from the National Action Network Convention on SiriusXM Progress 127.

"I was really honored by that, and I think our listeners were too, because from my point of view, if you're hosting a show, and a candidate says, "Hey, I want to come sit in your studio and talk to your audience," that is not just about you, that person's saying they value your audience and your listeners," says Thompson. She explained to him three of the issues that she has been working on since the start of her political career on that program:

> *HARRIS: The reality of and the prevalence of undiagnosed and untreated trauma among children—and adults—who are living in communities where there is poverty and/or violence, and they're usually the same community. And we have got to address that. It is a real issue. There is a phenomenal sister named Dr. Nadine Burke-Harris—no*

relation; she and I worked together for years on this issue. Which is studying, and then treating this, because it will have lifelong and generational consequence, if we don't address it as a very serious impediment. It's almost like a physical barrier to growth and development if we don't address trauma. And when we're looking at what happened with [slain Los Angeles rapper] Nipsey Hussle, and what happens every day in America, in communities; in particular in black communities. We are looking at lives being slaughtered at such a young age, and the entire community grieves and mourns. So there is that piece about trauma and what we need to do to address it.

There is the piece about gun violence. Let me tell you Mark, one of the things that drives me crazy, is the failure of so-called leaders in Washington, DC to have the courage to deal with this issue, and deal with it in a rational way. Right? There are so many leaders who fail to have the courage to reject the false choice which suggests you're either in favor of the Second Amendment or you want to take everyone's guns away. You want to go hunting, that's fine. But look, we need reasonable gun safety laws; which includes the need, the desperate need for universal background checks. The desperate need to renew the assault weapons ban . . .

And then, there is what we need to do to recognize that we have got to address the need for economic health and wellbeing in these communities where we are seeing violence. People have got to be very clear. There is a direct connection. . . . It is preventable. We can address it. There needs to be economic opportunities that are focused on these communities. A lot of what I am proposing as a candidate for president of the United States is directed at addressing the economic needs of communities that have for too long been neglected.

THOMPSON: You were a prosecutor, however there are some who are critical of the fact that you were a prosecutor. The civil rights movement fought for you to be in law enforcement; we need African Americans in law enforcement. But then as DuBois says, sometimes we have that "double-consciousness;" there is that historical tension between African Americans and law enforcement. So, how can you reconcile that within your own community. . . . By the same token, you get the tension that exists between African Americans and law enforcement.

HARRIS: Of course. There is that tension, and listen; my knowledge of that tension that began the day I was born. I didn't have to read about it. I didn't have to learn about it. I lived it. And, it was for that reason that I decided to be a prosecutor. Because I decided, look, we have got to be on the inside. Not only on the outside, but on the inside, where the power is; where the decisions are being

*made, to reform the system. And so that's what I chose
to do. It was a very conscious decision . . . .*[25]

"There are going to be some push and pull people are going to have in their own minds, but I think at the end of the day, she has been a person in criminal justice who has advocated for criminal justice reform as much, or more than any other person in that field," says Thompson, who is a pioneer in the field of satellite radio broadcasting since starting his program in 2001. "You can't run for attorney general in a state, you can't be a prosecutor running for office as a woman in particular, on a platform of complete overhaul and abolition of the criminal justice system." He continued:

*She told me stories about how even within the African
American community, there were demands for more
prosecution, more risk, because African Americans live in
fear of their own lives. She and I reminisce about all,
people talk about all this music now, but there used to be
a song by Public Enemy called, "9-1-1 is a Joke," which
was as much about the police killing African Americans,
as it was about police or law enforcement not being con-
cerned about addressing crime in the black community.*

*She's been on both sides, but she was a prosecutor.
I think that the challenge for people, is that as much as
we want criminal justice reform, criminal justice reform
includes people of diverse backgrounds, people who*

represent diversity in the roles of attorney general, and chiefs of police, and correctional officers, everything else.

Thompson explained that Senator Harris has a very solid base of support in a key swing voting bloc, black women. He believes that the former prosecutor will also pick up another significant block of female voters because, "my experience has been that Kamala's performance in the Kavanaugh hearings won her a lot of votes of white women. That's what I've been hearing, that's what I've heard on my show, that's what I've heard out on the trail, and in the community." He also explained that Kamala Harris's campaign will be significantly different from Hillary Clinton's campaign—though many of her advisers, including her campaign chairwoman, were on that 2016 endeavor—because the former secretary of state was so relentlessly attacked that she was on the defensive from the beginning. But, "if Kamala Harris were to win the nomination. . . . if the president were to start attacking her in the way he attacked Hillary and others, I think it would hurt Trump even further."[26]

The 2020 Democratic primary race is going to go on for thirteen months before the first votes are cast in New Hampshire's primary, some time before February 11, 2020. Primary campaigns are dynamic by their nature, and most often the early front-runner does not capture the party's nomination.

Kamala Harris will have to flesh out her campaign platform and take steps to satisfy the issues her critics are bound to cite during the 2016 campaign. She starts with a tremendous advantage in name recognition, funding, and supporters compared to most of her eighteen opponents.

A *RealClearPolitics* average of the polling for a head-to-head matchup between Donald Trump and Harris shows her winning narrowly, but the results vary wildly as of April 2019, from a seven-point margin in her favor according to Public Policy Polling to a tie with Emerson's poll and Fox News polling showing that Harris would lose by 2 percent.[27]

Harris has an objectively good chance of becoming the Democratic nominee in 2020, but she will have to distinguish himself from a large field, many of whom will likely try to push her on the details of her prosecutorial career. The senator's biggest hurdle is what happens if she wins a plurality of votes, but not a majority going into the Democratic National Convention, which would lead to a "brokered convention."[28] She's very likely to be asked to be another candidate's running mate if she doesn't succeed in the primary, because she easily would fill the "attack dog" role traditionally adopted by vice presidential candidates.

Kamala Harris can win the Democratic nomination. She would become only the second state attorney general to ascend to the presidency. The first, Bill Clinton, was also a Democrat and he won an election in recent times, so there is a precedent. Harris's skillfully delivered rhetoric and her inexorable rise from prosecutor to senator will provide the narrative of her campaign. Her policy focus on justice issues and helping America's middle class, while ensuring that impoverished communities—many of them of color—are not forgotten will make her a formidable candidate throughout the Democratic primary elections, and, possibly, in the general election.

NOTES

INTRODUCTION TO KAMALA HARRIS BY SERIES EDITOR SCOTT DWORKIN

1. Nichols, Chris. "'Examining Kamala Harris' Middle-Class Tax Cut Plan." *PolitiFact* California. Last modified March 24, 2019. www.politifact.com/california/article/2019/apr/11/kamala-harris-calls-her-lift-plan-most-significant/.

2. Mallenbaum, Carly. "Here's How Sen. Kamala Harris Answers Questions About 'Women's Issues.'" *USA Today*. Last modified June 14, 2017. www.usatoday.com/story/life/entertainthis/2017/06/14/kamala-harris-women-in-film/102837716/.

3. Lawler, Ophelia G. "One of Kamala Harris's Abortion Questions Left Kavanaugh Speechless." *The Cut*. Last modified September 5, 2018. www.thecut.com/2018/09/kamala-harriss-abortion-questions-left-kavanaugh-speechless.html.

4. Beauchamp, Zack. "The Mueller Report's Collusion Section Is Much Worse than You Think." *Vox*. Last modified April 18, 2019. www.vox.com/2019/4/18/18484965/mueller-report-trump-no-collusion.

5. Mazzetti, Mark. "Mueller Reveals Trump's Efforts to Thwart Russian Inquiry in Highly Anticipated Report." *New York Times*. Last modified April 18, 2019. www.nytimes.com/2019/04/18/us/politics/mueller-report-russian-interference-donald-trump.html.

6. Harris, Kamala. "Our America." The Accessed April 23, 2019. kamalaharris.org/our-america/.

7. Schwartz, Brian. "Cory Booker, Kamala Harris and Other Dems Reach Out to Wall Street to Gauge Possible 2020 Support." CNBC. Last modified January 8, 2019. www.cnbc.com/2019/01/07/wall-street-and-new-york-business-execs-gear-up-for-2020-presidential-election-html.

8. "Sen. Kamala D Harris - California." OpenSecrets. Accessed April 23, 2019. www.opensecrets.org/members-of-congress/industries?cid=N00036915&cycle=2018&type=I.

9. Harris, Kamala D. "Harris Statement Opposing Bill to Deregulate Big Banks." Last modified March 14, 2018. www.harris.senate.gov/news/press-releases/harris-statement-opposing-bill-to-deregulate-big-banks.

10. Harris, Kamala D. "Attorney General Kamala D. Harris Urges the Consumer Financial Protection Bureau to Adopt Consumer Protections against Harmful Practices by Payday Lenders." Last modified July 20, 2016. oag.ca.gov/news/press-releases/attorney-general-kamala-d-harris-urges-consumer-financial-protection-bureau.

11. Harris, Kamala. "Kamala Comments on Consumer Financial Protection Bureau." Twitter. Accessed April 23, 2019. twitter.com/SenKamalaHarris/status/935249229341175808.

12. Haeder, Simon F., and Susan W. Yackee. "The Trump administration might be deregulating more than you know (or could know)." *Washington Post*. Last modified August 24, 2018. www.washingtonpost.com/news/monkey-cage/wp/2018/08/24/the-trump-administration-might-be-deregulating-more-than-you-know-or-could-know/?utm_term=.e13fc03bb0a0.

13. Pew Research Center Social & Demographic Trends Project. Last modified October 25, 2018. www.pewsocialtrends.org/2017/06/22/the-demographics-of-gun-ownership/.

14.   Lah, Kyung. "Kamala Harris Talks About Owning a Gun: 'I Was a Career Prosecutor.'" CNN. Last modified April 11, 2019. www.cnn.com/2019/04/11/politics/kamala-harris-gun-owner /index.html.

15.   Harris, Kamala. "Action on Gun Violence in Kamala Harris First 100 Days." The Accessed April 23, 2019. kamalaharris.org/gunviolence/.

16.   Cadelago, Christopher. "Kamala Harris Launches Campaign for President." *Politico.* Last modified January 21, 2019. www.Politico.com/story/2019/01/21/kamala-harris-2020-campaign-1116076.

17.   Strauss, Daniel. "Buttigieg Plans Aggressive Fund-raising Push in California." *Politico.* Last modified April 19, 2019. www.Politico.com/story/2019/04/19/buttigieg-fund-raising-california -1282196.

18.   "Sen. Kamala Harris–California." OpenSecrets. Accessed April 23, 2019. www.opensecrets.org /members-of-congress/industries?cid=N00036915&cycle=CAREER&type=I.

19.   Ibid.

20.   Marinucci, Carla. "Harris Unveils California Endorsements in Home State Show of Force." *Politico.* Last modified February 7, 2019. www.Politico.com/story/2019/02/07/kamala-harris -2020-california-endorsments-1157651.

21.   Lovegrove, Jamie. "2020 Candidate Kamala Harris Picks Up Endorsements from 5 SC Democrats." *Post and Courier.* Last modified March 28, 2019. www.postandcourier.com /politics/candidate-kamala-harris-picks-up-endorsements-from-sc-democrats/article_229e192a -50d4-11e9-a1d7-df7e8109c2c7.html.

WHO IS KAMALA HARRIS?

1.   All bibliographical references to events in Chapter 2, including this interview with Mark Thompson are distributed throughout the rest of this book.

DEFINING MOMENTS IN HARRIS'S POLITICAL CAREER

1.   Afkhami, Artin. "Sessions Changes His Story on Russian Contacts in Senate Testimony." *Just Security.* Last modified December 3, 2018. www.justsecurity.org/46081/changes-story-russian -contacts-congress/.

2.   Harris, Kamala. Twitter. Accessed April 22, 2019. twitter.com/KamalaHarris/status /799771130802372608.

3.   "Kamala Harris Questions Attorney General Jeff Sessions." YouTube. June 13, 2017. Accessed April 22, 2019. www.youtube.com/watch?v=TCu1iIMRB30.

4.   Harris, Kamala. Twitter. Accessed April 22, 2019. twitter.com/KamalaHarris/status /874732172988567553.

5.   Estepa, Jessica. "Social Media Lights Up After Kamala Harris Questions Jeff Sessions." *USA Today.* Last modified June 13, 2017. www.usatoday.com/story/news/politics/onpolitics/2017 /06/13/social-media-lights-up-after-kamala-harris-questions-jeff-sessions/102824106/.

6.   Reid, Joy. Twitter. Accessed April 22, 2019. twitter.com/JoyAnnReid/status/874728850160308224.

7.   Bendery, Jennifer. Twitter. Accessed April 22, 2019. twitter.com/jbendery/status /874729195867340801.

8.   Estepa, Jessica. "Social Media Lights Up After Kamala Harris Questions Jeff Sessions." *USA Today.* Last modified June 13, 2017. www.usatoday.com/story/news/politics/onpolitics/2017 /06/13/social-media-lights-up-after-kamala-harris-questions-jeff-sessions/102824106/.

9. Rubin, Jennifer. "Here's why we need to know how Kavanaugh got on Trump's Supreme Court list." *Washington Post.* Last modified August 3, 2018. www.washingtonpost.com/blogs/right-turn/wp/2018/08/03/heres-why-we-need-to-know-how-kavanaugh-got-on-trumps-supreme-court-list/.

10. Senate Judiciary Hearing on the nomination of Judge Brett Kavanaugh to the US Supreme Court, Thursday, September 5, 2018.

11. Ibid.

12. Ibid.

13. Siskind, Amy. Twitter. Accessed April 22, 2019. twitter.com/Amy_Siskind/status/1037774038280617984.

14. Senate Democrats. Twitter. Accessed April 22, 2019. twitter.com/SenateDems/status/1037524715403993088.

15. Bort, Ryan. "Kamala Harris and Cory Booker Have Upended the Kavanaugh Hearings." *Rolling Stone.* Last modified September 6, 2018. www.rollingstone.com/politics/politics-news/kamala-harris-cory-booker-kavanaugh-719776/.

16. Durkin D. AP News. Accessed April 22, 2019. twitter.com/jiveDurkey/status/1037715530206130177.

17. *The Rachel Maddow Show.* September 6, 2018. TV program. MSNBC.

18. Brackets are labeled (audio gap) in transcript, but that is the issue which would cause a judge to recuse themselves, the appearance of partiality in a case.

19. Brown, Emma. "California Professor, Writer of Confidential Brett Kavanaugh Letter, Speaks Out about Her Allegation of Sexual Assault." *Washington Post.* Last modified September 16, 2018. www.washingtonpost.com/investigations/california-professor-writer-of-confidential-brett-kavanaugh-letter-speaks-out-about-her-allegation-of-sexual-assault/2018/09/16/46982194-b846-11e8-94eb-3bd52dfe917b_story.html.

20. *CBS This Morning.* September 18, 2018. TV program. CBS.

21. Chamberlain, Samuel. "Kavanaugh Denies Sexual Misconduct in Fox News Exclusive: 'I Know I'm telling the Truth.'" Fox News. Last modified September 24, 2018. www.foxnews.com/politics/kavanaugh-denies-sexual-misconduct-in-fox-news-exclusive-i-know-im-telling-the-truth.

22. Swoyer, Alex. "Two Ethics Complaints Filed Against Brett Kavanaugh." *Washington Times.* Last modified October 2, 2018. www.washingtontimes.com/news/2018/oct/2/two-ethics-complaints-filed-against-brett-kavanaug/.

23. Disclosure: Scott Dworkin is a cofounder of the Democratic Coalition.

24. Senate Judiciary Hearing on the nomination of Judge Brett Kavanaugh to the US Supreme Court, Thursday, September 27, 2018.

25. Ibid.

26. Bump, Philip. "Kavanaugh is pressed on the key July 1 entry in his calendar. But only to a point." *Washington Post.* Last modified September 28, 2018. www.washingtonpost.com/politics/2018/09/27/kavanaugh-is-pressed-key-july-entry-his-calendar-only-point/.

27. Bump, Philip. "Mark Judge's book validates Christine Blasey Ford's timeline of the alleged Kavanaugh assault." *Washington Post.* Last modified September 27, 2018. www.washingtonpost.com/politics/2018/09/27/mark-judges-book-validates-christine-fords-timeline-alleged-kavanaugh-assault/?utm_term=.3f856b1e6aff.

28. Zhou, Li. "The Entry on Brett Kavanaugh's Calendar That Could Matter, Explained." *Vox.* Last modified September 28, 2018. www.vox.com/policy-and-politics/2018/9/28/17914174/brett-kavanaugh-calendar-christine-blasey-ford.

29. Lopez, German. "The FBI's Limited Investigation into the Kavanaugh Sexual Assault Allegations, Explained." *Vox*. Last modified October 3, 2018. www.vox.com/policy-and-politics /2018/10/1/17916254/kavanaugh-fbi-investigation-ford-trump.

30. Ting, Eric. "Kamala Harris Unloads on 'Unfit' Kavanaugh, White House in Fiery Senate Floor Speech." *SFGate*. Last modified October 5, 2018. www.sfgate.com/politics/article/Kamala -Harris-Kavanaugh-White-House-FBI-speech-13285239.php.

31. Silverstein, Jason. "Brett Kavanaugh Confirmed to Supreme Court by Smallest Margin Since 1881." CBSNews.com. Last modified October 6, 2018. www.cbsnews.com/news/brett-kavanaugh -confirmed-to-supreme-court-by-smallest-margin-in-modern-history/.

32. Kelly, Caroline. "FBI Director: Kavanaugh Background Probe 'Limited in Scope.'" CNN. Last modified October 10, 2018. www.cnn.com/2018/10/10/politics/fbi-wray-kavanaugh-ford-probe /index.html.

33. Hensley-Clancy, Molly. "Kamala Harris Has Cult Status in Iowa after the Kavanaugh Hearings." *BuzzFeed News*. Last modified October 24, 2018. www.buzzfeednews.com/article /mollyhensleyclancy/kamala-harris-iowa-2020-campaign-brett-kavanaugh.

34. Harris, Kamala. "Christine Blasey Ford Is on the 2019 TIME 100 List.com." Time.com. Accessed April 22, 2019. time.com/collection/100-most-influential-people-2019/5567675 /christine-blasey-ford/.

35. Carney, Jordain. "Trump, GOP Aim to Weaponize Kavanaugh Vote Ahead of November." *The Hill*. Last modified October 7, 2018. thehill.com/homenews/campaign/410245-trump-gop-aim -to-weaponize-kavanaugh-vote-ahead-of-november.

CAMPAIGN PLATFORM

1. The EITC is a "refundable tax credit," which means that even someone who does not owe taxes can claim the credit, which is why it is sometimes known as a negative income tax. This is similar to a universal basic income (UBI), which provides cash payments to every citizen, but the EITC is income tested and therefore not universal.

2. Martin, Jonathan. "For Kamala Harris, a Strong Start, but with Some Notable Stumbles." *New York Times*. Last modified February 27, 2019. www.nytimes.com/2019/02/26/us/politics/kamala -harris-president-2020.html.

3. Crandall-Hollick, Margot. "The Earned Income Tax Credit (EITC): A Brief Legislative History." Federation of American Scientists. Accessed April 24, 2019. fas.org/sgp/crs/misc/R44825.pdf.

4. "President Clinton Proposes to Expand the Earned Income Tax Credit." Welcome To The White House. Accessed April 24, 2019. clintonwhitehouse4.archives.gov/WH/New/html /20000112_2.html.

5. "American Recovery and Reinvestment Act of 2009." Wikipedia. Accessed April 24, 2019. en.wikipedia.org/wiki/American_Recovery_and_Reinvestment_Act_of_2009.

6. Lowrey, Annie. "Kamala Harris's Trump-Size Tax Plan." *The Atlantic*. Last modified October 18, 2018. www.theatlantic.com/ideas/archive/2018/10/lefts-trump-sized-tax-plans/573328/.

7. Wilson, Valerie, and Jessica Schieder. "Countries Investing More in Social Programs Have Less Child Poverty." Economic Policy Institute. Accessed April 24, 2019. www.epi.org/publication /countries-investing-more-in-social-programs-have-less-child-poverty/.

8. Maag, Elaine. "Senator Harris Seeks to Raise Incomes Using a New Tax Credit." Tax Policy Center. Last modified October 18, 2018. www.taxpolicycenter.org/taxvox/senator-harris-seeks -raise-incomes-using-new-tax-credit.

9. Grayer, Annie, and Kyung Lah. "Inside Kamala Harris' Plan to Raise Teacher Salaries." CNN. Last modified March 26, 2019. www.cnn.com/2019/03/26/politics/kamala-harris-teacher -salaries-proposal/index.html.

10. Rios, Edwin. "Kamala Harris' Big Plan for Teacher Pay Is Promising 'But It'd Require a Major Change for How the Feds Handle Education." *Mother Jones.* Last modified March 29, 2019. www.motherjones.com/politics/2019/03/kamala-harris-teacher-pay-gap-democrat-plan/.

11. Startz, Dick. "Opinion: Teacher Raises Will Pay for Themselves." *Newsday.* Last modified April 23, 2019. www.newsday.com/opinion/commentary/teacher-raises-kamala-harris-educators-1.30152564.

12. Grayer, Annie, and Kyung Lah. "Inside Kamala Harris' Plan to Raise Teacher Salaries." CNN. Last modified March 26, 2019. www.cnn.com/2019/03/26/politics/kamala-harris-teacher -salaries-proposal/index.html. - Ibid 9.

13. Harris, Kamala. "College for All." *Medium.* Last modified April 3, 2017. medium.com /@KamalaHarris/college-for-all-b09f63b82cd.

14. Cadelago, Christopher. "Kamala Harris Proposes Major Executive Actions to Crack Down on Guns." *Politico.* Last modified April 22, 2019. www.Politico.com/story/2019/04/22/kamala -harris-guns-town-hall-1287205.

15. Lemon, Don. "CNN Hosts a Town Hall with Sen. Kamala Harris (D-CA) Presidential Candidate." CNN. April 22nd, 2019.

16. Kurtzleben, Danielle. "Here's What's in Bernie Sanders' 'Medicare For All' Bill." NPR.org. Last modified September 14, 2017. www.npr.org/2017/09/14/550768280/heres-whats-in-bernie -sanders-medicare-for-all-bill.

17. "Sanders, 14 Senators Introduce Medicare for All." Last modified April 10, 2019. www.sanders .senate.gov/newsroom/press-releases/sanders-14-senators-introduce-medicare-for-all.

18. Lemon, Don, op. cit.

19. "National Health Expenditure Trends, 1975 to 2015." Canadian Institute for Health Information. Accessed April 24, 2019. secure.cihi.ca/free_products/nhex_trends_narrative_report_2015_en.pdf.

20. Volsky, Igor. "Can Canadians Purchase Private Health Insurance Coverage?" *ThinkProgress.* Accessed April 24, 2019. thinkprogress.org/can-canadians-purchase-private-health-insurance -coverage-ed7a25f9c602/.

21. "Amid Rising Costs of Housing, Harris Introduces Bill to Provide Rent Relief." Last modified July 19, 2018. www.harris.senate.gov/news/press-releases/amid-rising-costs-of-housing-harris -introduces-bill-to-provide-rent-relief.

22. Dorfman, Jeffrey. "Democrats Proposed Rent Subsidy Would Enrich Landlords and Fleece Taxpayers." *Forbes.* Last modified July 22, 2018. www.forbes.com/sites/jeffreydorfman/2018/07 /22/democrats-proposed-rent-subsidy-would-enrich-landlords-and-fleece-taxpayers/#571c4adbac05.

23. "Harris Reintroduces Legislation to Provide Relief to Americans Facing Skyrocketing Cost of Rent." Last modified April 9, 2019. www.harris.senate.gov/news/press-releases/harris -reintroduces-legislation-to-provide-relief-to-americans-facing-skyrocketing-cost-of-rent.

24. S.1593 —115th Congress (2017–2018).

25. "ACLU Comment on the Introduction of the Pretrial Integrity and Safety Act, a Federal Bail Reform Bill." American Civil Liberties Union. Accessed April 24, 2019. www.aclu.org/news /aclu-comment-introduction-pretrial-integrity-and-safety-act-federal-bail-reform-bill-1.

26. Harris, Kamala, and Rand Paul. "To Shrink Jails, Let's Reform Bail." *New York Times.* Last modified January 20, 2018. www.nytimes.com/2017/07/20/opinion/kamala-harris-and-rand -paul-lets-reform-bail.html.

27. Eli Watkins. "Senate Passes Bill Making Lynching a Federal Crime." CNN. Last modified December 19, 2018. www.cnn.com/2018/12/19/politics/senate-anti-lynching/index.html.

28. "Justice for Victims of Lynching Act of 2019 (S. 488)." GovTrack.us. Accessed April 24, 2019. www.govtrack.us/congress/bills/116/s488.

29. "Harris Reintroduces Legislation to Protect Civil Rights of All Americans." Last modified February 28, 2019. www.harris.senate.gov/news/press-releases/harris-reintroduces-legislation-to -protect-civil-rights-of-all-americans.

30. "Harris, Merkley, Cortez Masto Introduce Bill to Reunify and Protect Immigrant Families." U.S. Senator Kamala Harris of California. Last modified July 17, 2018. www.harris.senate.gov /news/press-releases/harris-merkley-cortez-masto-introduce-bill-to-reunify-and-protect-immigrant -families.

31. Lemon, Don, op. cit.

32. "Harris, Merkley, Cortez Masto Introduce Bill to Reunify and Protect Immigrant Families."

33. "Harris Bill to Preserve and Improve Historic HBCU Buildings and Sites Passes Senate." U.S. Senator Kamala Harris of California. Last modified February 12, 2019. www.harris.senate.gov /news/press-releases/harris-bill-to-preserve-and-improve-historic-hbcu-buildings-and-sites-passes -senate.

34. "Text - S.47 - 116th Congress (2019-2020): John D. Dingell, Jr. Conservation, Management, and Recreation Act." Congress.gov | Library of Congress. Last modified March 12, 2019. www .congress.gov/bill/116th-congress/senate-bill/47/text.

35. Harris, Kamala. Twitter. Accessed April 24, 2019. twitter.com/KamalaHarris/status /915288344300572673.

36. Starr, Terrell J. "Exclusive: Kamala Harris Calls for Decriminalization of Sex Work, Unequivocally Calls Trump a Racist and Wants Reparations (Sort Of)." *The Root.* Last modified February 26, 2019. www.theroot.com/exclusive-kamala-harris-calls-for-decriminalization-of-1832883951.

FORMATIVE BACKGROUND AND EDUCATION

1. Legacy.com. Obituary: Shyamala Harris. Accessed April 19, 2019. www.legacy.com/obituaries /sfgate/obituary.aspx?pid=125330757.

2. "Sen. Kamala Harris Announces 2020 Presidential Run." YouTube. January 21, 2019. www .youtube.com/watch?v=Frt81nmSbz8.

3. "Professional Career." Stanford University. Accessed April 19, 2019. web.stanford.edu/~dharris /professional_career.htm.

4. Halper, Evan. "A Political Awakening: How Howard University Shaped Kamala Harris, Identity." *Los Angeles Times.* Last modified March 19, 2019. www.latimes.com/politics/la-na-pol-kamala -harris-howard-university-20190319-story.html.

5. Owens, Donna. "California Attorney General Kamala Harris Plans to Be America's Next Black Female Senator." *Essence.* Last modified January 13, 2016. www.essence.com/news/california -attorney-general-kamala-harris-americas-next-black-female-senator/.

6. Harris, Kamala, with Joan O'C Hamilton. *Smart on Crime: A Career Prosecutor's Plan to Make Us Safer.* San Francisco, Calif: Chronicle Books, 2009.

7. McCarten, James. "Kamala Harris, Schooled in Montreal, Announces Bid to Unseat Trump in 2020." Global News. Last modified January 21, 2019. globalnews.ca/news/4872687/kamala -harris-montreal-2020-presidential-race/.

8. "Rising Democratic Party Star Kamala Harris Has Montreal Roots." *CTV News*. Last modified October 9, 2017. www.ctvnews.ca/canada/rising-democratic-party-star-kamala-harris-has -montreal-roots-1.3625032.

9. Dzieza, Josh. "Legal Power Sisters Credit Mom." *The Daily Beast*. Last modified March 10, 2012. www.thedailybeast.com/legal-power-sisters-credit-mom.

10. Dale, Daniel. "U.S. Sen. Kamala Harris's Classmates from Her Canadian High School Cheer Her Potential Run for President." *Toronto Star*. Last modified December 29, 2018. www.thestar .com/news/world/2018/12/29/kamala-harriss-classmates-from-her-canadian-high-school-cheer -her-campaign-for-us-president.html.

11. Also known as one of the HBCUs, which stands for historically black colleges and universities

12. "Howard University: Historically Black Colleges and Universities." Wikipedia, Last modified November 11, 2003. en.wikipedia.org/wiki/List_of_historically_black_colleges_and_universities.

13. Halper, Evan. "A Political Awakening: How Howard University Shaped Kamala Harris, Identity." *Los Angeles Times*. Last modified March 19, 2019. www.latimes.com/politics/la-na-pol-kamala -harris-howard-university-20190319-story.html.

14. Reston, Maeve. "Kamala Harris' Secret Weapon: The Sisters of AKA." CNN. Last modified January 27, 2019. www.cnn.com/2019/01/24/politics/kamala-harris-sorority-sisters-south -carolina/index.html.

15. Hamilton, Kerry-Ann. "Howard Alumna Trailblazer Becomes First Woman Elected As California Attorney General." *Howard University Newsroom*. Last modified December 14, 2010. web.archive.org/web/20110112015549/www.howard.edu/newsroom/releases /2010/20101215HowardAlumnaTrailblazerBecomesFirstWomanElectedasCaliforniaAttorney General.html.

16. Harold, Fisher. "Kamala Harris Discusses Presidential Run at Howard University, Winter Storm Hits East." WHUR 96.3 FM. Last modified January 21, 2019. whur.com/news/kamala-harris -discusses-presidential-run-at-howard-university-winter-storm-hits-east/.

17. Kaplan, Steve. "Brilliant Careers." Super Lawyers. Last modified March 22, 2018. www .superlawyers.com/california-northern/article/brilliant-careers/e8902c40-542b-40e4-89a5 -58a2e181b36f.html.

18. "Kamala Devi Harris #146672 - Attorney Search." My State Bar Profile: The State Bar of California. Accessed April 19, 2019. members.calbar.ca.gov/fal/Licensee/Detail/146672.

19. Meth, Madeline. "Maya Harris Joins the Center for American Progress as Senior Fellow." Center for American Progress. Last modified October 29, 2013. www.americanprogress.org/press /release/2013/10/29/78308/release-maya-harris-joins-the-center-for-american-progress-as -senior-fellow/.

20. Glueck, Katie. "The Power Players behind Hillary Clinton's Campaign." *Politico*. Last modified June 30, 2015. www.Politico.com/story/2015/04/hillary-clintons-power-players-116874.

21. Greenhouse, Emily. "Meet Maya Harris, Hillary Clinton's Progressive Link." *New Yorker*. Last modified November 5, 2016. www.newyorker.com/news/news-desk/meet-maya-harris-hillary -clintons-progressive-link.

22. King, Jamila. "Can Harris' Sister Help Her Overcome the "Kamala Is a Cop" Rap?" *Mother Jones*. Last modified February 13, 2019. www.motherjones.com/politics/2019/02/kamala-maya -harris-progressive-prosecutor-campaign-criminal-justice/.

23. "Tony and Maya: Partners in Public Service." Stanford Law School. Accessed April 19, 2019. law.stanford.edu/stanford-lawyer/articles/tony-and-maya-partners-in-public-service/.

24. Cockerham, Sean. "Sen.-elect Kamala Harris Picks Top Deputy in California Attorney General's Office as Her Chief of Staff." *McClatchy DC Bureau.* Last modified November 30, 2016. www.mcclatchydc.com/news/politicsgovernment/congress/article117988773.html.

25. Trickey, Erick. "Meena Harris' 12." *Harvard Law Today.* Last modified January 29, 2019. today. law.harvard.edu/meena-harris-12/.

26. Joseph, Cameron. "Sister Action: Kamala and Maya Harris Tag-Team The Fight For The White House." *Talking Points Memo.* Last modified April 12, 2019. talkingpointsmemo.com/dc/maya -harris-sister-kamala-harris-campaign-chairman.

27. "Community-Centered Policing: A Force for Change." PolicyLink. Last modified January 2001. www.policylink.org/resources-tools/community-centered-policing-a-force-for-change.

28. Joseph, Cameron. "Sister Action: Kamala and Maya Harris Tag-Team The Fight For The White House." *Talking Points Memo.* Last modified April 12, 2019. talkingpointsmemo.com/dc/maya -harris-sister-kamala-harris-campaign-chairman.

29. Harris, Scott D. "In Search of Elusive Justice." *Los Angeles Times.* Last modified October 24, 2004. www.latimes.com/politics/la-pol-ca-tm-kamala-20190121-story.html.

30. Byrne, Peter. "Kamala's Karma - September 24, 2003." *SF Weekly.* Last modified September 24, 2003. www.sfweekly.com/news/kamalas-karma/.

31. "Kamala Harris." Truman Center. Accessed April 19, 2019. trumancenter.org/team-view/kamala -harris/.

32. "Biography: Kamala Harris for DA." Wayback Machine. Accessed April 19, 2019. web.archive. org/web/20041119160806/www.kamalaharris.org/about/biography;jsessionid =FVBHOSTWDJPL0CQQPABCFEY.

33. Harris, Scott D. "In Search of Elusive Justice." *Los Angeles Times.* Last modified October 24, 2004. www.latimes.com/politics/la-pol-ca-tm-kamala-20190121-story.html.

34. "Biography: Kamala Harris for DA." Wayback Machine. Accessed April 19, 2019. web.archive. org/web/20041119160806/www.kamalaharris.org/about/biography;jsessionid =FVBHOSTWDJPL0CQQPABCFEY.

35. "District Attorney; City of San Francisco Election Information December 9, 2003 Election." Voter's Edge California. Last modified December 9, 2003. www.smartvoter.org/2003/12/09/ca /sf/race/2/.

36. "Kamala Harris for DA." Wayback Machine January 8, 2004. Accessed April 19, 2019. web. archive.org/web/20040210113616/www.kamalaharris.org/.

37. Kampeas, JTA R. "5 Jewish Facts about Kamala Harris." *Jewish News of Northern California.* Last modified January 14, 2019. www.jweekly.com/2019/01/14/5-jewish-facts-about-kamala -harris/.

38. Kurtz, Judy. "Kamala Harris: 'Single Women in Politics' Aren't Granted the Same 'Latitude' as Men." *The Hill.* Last modified January 8, 2019. thehill.com/blogs/in-the-know/in-the-know /424344-kamala-harris-single-women-in-politics-arent-granted-the-same.

CAREER AS SAN FRANCISCO DISTRICT ATTORNEY

1. Nittle, Nadra K. "This Groundbreaking Senator Has Been Called the Female Barack Obama." *ThoughtCo.* Last modified February 10, 2019. www.thoughtco.com/california-attorney-general -kamala-harris-2834885.

2. "Kamala Harris for DA: Domestic Violence." Wayback Machine. Accessed April 19, 2019. web.archive.org/web/20031230014709/www.kamalaharris.org/about/issues/domesticviolence/.

3. "Kamala Harris for DA: Issues." Wayback Machine. Accessed April 19, 2019. web.archive.org /web/20031213112412/www.kamalaharris.org/about/issues/.

4. Ballotpedia. "California Proposition 21, Treatment of Juvenile Offenders (2000)." Ballotpedia. Accessed April 19, 2019. ballotpedia.org/California_Proposition_21,Treatment_of_Juvenile _Offenders_(2000).

5. "Biography: Kamala Harris for DA." Wayback Machine. Accessed April 19, 2019. web.archive .org/web/20041119160806/www.kamalaharris.org/about/biography;jsessionid =FVBHOSTWDJPL0CQQPABCFEY.

6. Byrne, Peter. "Kamala's Karma - September 24, 2003." *SF Weekly.* Last modified September 24, 2003. www.sfweekly.com/news/kamalas-karma/.

7. Toobin, Jeffrey. "After Fajita gate." *New Yorker.* Accessed April 19, 2019. www.newyorker.com /magazine/2003/07/14/after-fajitagate.

8. Gordon, Rachel. "Harris Violated S.F. Campaign Finance Law / D.A. Candidate to Pay Up to $34,000 for 'unintentional' Mistake." *SFGate.* Last modified October 7, 2003. www.sfgate.com /politics/article/Harris-violated-S-F-campaign-finance-law-D-A-2554388.php.

9. Fang, Lee. "In Her First Race, Kamala Harris Campaigned As Tough on Crime—and Unseated the Country's Most Progressive Prosecutor." *The Intercept.* Last modified February 7, 2019. theintercept.com/2019/02/07/kamala-harris-san-francisco-district-attorney-crime/.

10. Byrne, Peter. "Kamala's Karma - September 24, 2003." *SF Weekly.* Last modified September 24, 2003. www.sfweekly.com/news/kamalas-karma/.

11. "Kamala Harris." n.d. theintercept.imgix.net/wp-uploads/sites/1/2019/02/enough-is-enough -kamala-flyer-inside-1549561264.jpg.

12. Byrne, Peter. "Kamala's Karma - September 24, 2003." *SF Weekly.* Last modified September 24, 2003. www.sfweekly.com/news/kamalas-karma/.

13. Siders, David. "'Ruthless': How Kamala Harris Won Her First Race." *Politico.* Last modified January 24, 2019. www.Politico.com/magazine/story/2019/01/24/kamala-harris-2020-history -224126.

14. "District Attorney; City of San Francisco Election Information November 4, 2003 Election." Voter's Edge California. Last modified November 4, 2003. www.smartvoter.org/2003/11/04/ca /sf/race/2/.

15. Ibid.

16. Siders, David, op. cit.

17. Harris, Scott D. "In Search of Elusive Justice." *Los Angeles Times.* Last modified October 24, 2004. www.latimes.com/politics/la-pol-ca-tm-kamala-20190121-story.html.

18. Ibid.

19. "District Attorney Program is Now Statewide Example." *San Francisco Examiner.* Last modified October 14, 2009. www.sfexaminer.com/news/district-attorney-program-is-now-statewide -example/.

20. Harris, Kamala D. "Finding the Path Back on Track." *HuffPost.* Last modified May 25, 2011. www.huffpost.com/entry/finding-the-path-back-on_b_350679.

21. Winston, Ali. "Cover of Darkness: S.F. Police Turned a Blind Eye to Some of the City's Most Dangerous Criminals—Who Were Also Some of Their Most Trusted Sources." *SF Weekly.* Last modified May 8, 2013. www.sfweekly.com/news/cover-of-darkness-s-f-police-turned-a-blind

-eye-to-some-of-the-citys-most-dangerous-criminals-who-were-also-some-of-their-most-trusted
-sources/.

22. "Brady V. Maryland, 373 U.S. 83 (1963): Prosecutors have a mandatory duty to disclose any exculpatory evidence or impeachment material they possess." Wikipedia. Last modified April 3, 2019. en.wikipedia.org/wiki/Brady_v._Maryland.

23. Derbeken, Jaxon V. "Judge Rips Harris' Office for Hiding Problems." *SFGate*. Last modified May 21, 2010. www.sfgate.com/bayarea/article/Judge-rips-Harris-office-for-hiding-problems -3263797.php.

24. Elias, Paul, and Terry Collins. "SFPD Crime Lab Case from A-Z." *NBC Bay Area*. Last modified April 18, 2010. www.nbcbayarea.com/news/local/SFPD-Crime-Lab-Case-From-A-Z -91434379.html.

25. H.R. 933 - 110th Congress (2007-2008).

26. "Harris Testimony." Wayback Machine. Last modified April 24, 2007. web.archive.org /web/20180926205854/www.judiciary.house.gov/_files/hearings/April2007/Harris070424.pdf.

27. Knight, Heather. "Kamala Harris Celebrates Unopposed Bid for District Attorney." *SFGate*. Last modified November 7, 2007. www.sfgate.com/news/article/Kamala-Harris-celebrates -unopposed-bid-for-3301780.php.

28. "SF DA Wants Californians to Give Her a Promotion." *NBC Bay Area*. Last modified July 17, 2009. www.nbcbayarea.com/news/local/SF-DA-to-Run-for-Higher-Office.html.

29. Grant, Traci. "Ambitious SF Politician Targets Truant Teens." *NBC Bay Area*. Last modified September 25, 2009. www.nbcbayarea.com/news/local/San-Francisco-DA-Pushes-Parent -Punishment-61534042.html.

30. Lopez, German. "Why Kamala Harris is Under Attack for a Decade-Old Anti-Truancy Program." *Vox*. Last modified February 7, 2019. www.vox.com/future-perfect/2019/2/7/18202084 /kamala-harris-truancy-prosecutor-president-2020.

31. "The San Francisco Unified School District Fails to Enforce School Attendance." Doc player. net. Accessed April 19, 2019. docplayer.net/23489563-The-san-francisco-unified-school -district-fails-to-enforce-school-attendance.html.

32. "Tolerating Truancy – Inviting Failure: The San Francisco Unified School District Fails To Enforce School Attendance." San Francisco Civil Grand Jury. Last modified June 11, 2003. civilgrandjury.sfgov.org/2002_2003/Tolerating_Truancy_Inviting_Failure.pdf.

33. San Francisco Public Library. "Civil Grand Jury Reports." Accessed April 19, 2019. www .archive.org/stream/civilgrandjuryre200809cali/civilgrandjuryre200809cali_djvu.txt.

34. Harris, Kamala. "Truancy Costs Us All." *SFGate*. Last modified October 14, 2009. www.sfgate .com/education/article/Truancy-costs-us-all-3213456.php.

35. "Kamala Harris (1/14/10)." YouTube. January 29, 2010. www.youtube.com/watch?v =QKaCFmNefHA.

36. Macguill, Dab. "FACT CHECK: Did Kamala Harris Once Boast About Prosecuting a Homeless Mother?" Snopes.com. Last modified February 1, 2019. www.snopes.com/fact-check /kamala-harris-homeless-mother/.

37. Twitter. Accessed April 19, 2019.

38. "San Francisco Truancy Reduction Initiative: Plan to Increase Attendance." Last modified December 2011. web.archive.org/web/20150919100201/www.dcyf.org/modules/showdocument .aspx?documentid=1145.

39. Emerson, Kimberly M. "San Francisco D.A. Kamala Harris Talks to Kimberly Marteau about Her New Book *Smart on Crime*." *HuffPost*. Last modified December 6, 2017. www.huffpost .com/entry/san-francisco-da-kamala-h_b_369505.

40. Harris, Kamala, with Joan O'C Hamilton. *Smart on Crime: A Career Prosecutor's Plan to Make Us Safer*. San Francisco: Chronicle Books, 2009.

41. Clancy, Molly H. "The Dated Politics of Kamala Harris' Criminal Justice Book." *BuzzFeed News*. Last modified August 20, 2018. www.buzzfeednews.com/article/mollyhensleyclancy /kamala-harris-smart-on-crime-book.

42. Lopez, German. "There Are Huge Racial Disparities in How US Police Use Force." *Vox*. Last modified November 14, 2018. www.vox.com/identities/2016/8/13/17938186/police-shootings -killings-racism-racial-disparities.

43. Chung, Ed. "Smart on Crime: An Alternative to the Tough vs. Soft Debate." Center for American Progress. Last modified May 12, 2017. www.americanprogress.org/issues/criminal -justice/news/2017/05/12/432238/smart-crime-alternative-tough-vs-soft-debate/.

CALIFORNIA'S ATTORNEY GENERAL

1. "Gwen Ifill Discusses Kamala Harris." YouTube. March 25, 2009. Accessed April 20, 2019. www.youtube.com/watch?v=1JVWB3E9sn8.

2. "6 Democrats Vie for Votes in California's Crowded Attorney General Race." Southern California Public Radio. Last modified October 14, 2012. www.scpr.org/news/2010/06/01/15580 /six-democrats-vie-votes-californias-crowded-attorn/.

3. Davis, Teddy. "Kamala Harris, the 'Female Barack Obama,' Answers Her Critics." *ABC News*. Last modified November 27, 2009. abcnews.go.com/Politics/female-barack-obama-answers -critics/story?id=9178493.

4. "Brady V. Maryland, 373 U.S. 83 (1963): Prosecutors have a mandatory duty to disclose any exculpatory evidence or impeachment material they possess." Wikipedia. Last modified April 3, 2019. en.wikipedia.org/wiki/Brady_v._Maryland.

5. "Kamala Harris - Candidate for Attorney General." Southern California Public Radio. Last modified October 14, 2012. www.scpr.org/programs/airtalk/2010/05/27/13863/kamala-harris -candidate-for-attorney-general/.

6. "6 Democrats Vie for Votes in California's Crowded Attorney General Race." Southern California Public Radio. Last modified October 14, 2012. www.scpr.org/news/2010/06/01/15580 /six-democrats-vie-votes-californias-crowded-attorn/.

7. Olopade, Dayo. "Kamala Harris, the 'Female Obama,' Wins Primary for California Attorney General." *Daily Beast*. Last modified June 9, 2010. www.thedailybeast.com/kamala-harris-the -female-obama-wins-primary-for-california-attorney-general.

8. "Alberto Torrico." Wikipedia. Last modified February 11, 2007. en.wikipedia.org/wiki/Alberto _Torrico.

9. "Attorney General; Democratic Party Election Information June 8, 2010 Election." Voter's Edge California. Last modified June 8, 2010. www.smartvoter.org/2010/06/08/ca/state/race/atgend/.

10. Smith, Ben. "Kamala Harris: Democrats' Anti-Palin." *Politico*. Last modified December 26, 2010. www.Politico.com/story/2010/12/kamala-harris-democrats-anti-palin-046783.

11. Armentano, Paul. "Kamala Harris." *NORML Blog*. Last modified November 23, 2010. blog .norml.org/tag/kamala-harris/.

12. Hing, Julianne. "California Parents Could Get Jail Time if Kids Miss School." *Colorlines.* Last modified January 9, 2018. www.colorlines.com/articles/california-parents-could-get-jail-time-if-kids-miss-school.

13. Burns, Alexander. "California's High-Stakes AG Race." *Politico.* Last modified November 18, 2010. www.Politico.com/story/2010/11/californias-high-stakes-ag-race-045300.

14. Leonard, Jack, and Seema Meht. "Steve Cooley Concedes Race for Attorney General to Kamala Harris." *Los Angeles Times.* Last modified March 14, 2019. www.latimes.com/archives/la-xpm-2010-nov-25-la-me-cooley-20101125-story.html.

15. "Vice Presidential Candidacy of Sarah Palin." Wikipedia. Last modified March 14, 2012. en.wikipedia.org/wiki/Vice_presidential_candidacy_of_Sarah_Palin.

16. Smith, Ben, op. cit.

17. Thompson, Don. "California Swears in First Female Attorney General." *San Diego Union-Tribune.* Last modified January 3, 2011. www.sandiegouniontribune.com/sdut-california-swears-in-first-female-attorney-general-2011jan03-story.html.

18. Ibid.

19. Harris, Kamala D. "Attorney General Kamala D. Harris Inaugural Remark." Accessed April 20, 2019. ag.ca.gov/cms_attachments/press/pdfs/n2021_final_speech.pdf.

20. Redden, Molly. "The Human Costs of Kamala Harris' War on Truancy." *HuffPost.* Last modified March 29, 2019. www.huffpost.com/entry/kamala-harris-truancy-arrests-2020-progressive-prosecutor_n_5c995789e4b0f7bfa1b57d2e.

21. "The County: the Story of America's Deadliest Police." *The Guardian.* Last modified December 3, 2018. www.theguardian.com/us-news/2015/dec/01/the-county-kern-county-deadliest-police-killings.

22. Harris, Kamala D. "Attorney General Kamala D. Harris Kicks Off First-of-its-Kind Law Enforcement Training on Implicit Bias & Procedural Justice." Last modified July 20, 2016. oag.ca.gov/news/press-releases/attorney-general-kamala-d-harris-kicks-first-its-kind-law-enforcement-training.

23. Harris, Kamala. "Attorney General Kamala D. Harris Expands Implicit Bias and Procedural Justice Training to the California Highway Patrol." Last modified October 6, 2016. oag.ca.gov/news/press-releases/attorney-general-kamala-d-harris-expands-implicit-bias-and-procedural-justice.

24. Harris, Kamala D. "Attorney General Kamala D. Harris Launches First-of-Its-Kind Criminal Justice Open Data Initiative." Last modified July 20, 2016. oag.ca.gov/news/press-releases/attorney-general-kamala-d-harris-launches-first-its-kind-criminal-justice-open.

25. Addison, Janae. "How Kamala Harris' Record on Police Body Cameras Fits into the 2020 Debate on Criminal Justice." *PBS News Hour.* Last modified April 12, 2019. www.pbs.org/newshour/politics/how-kamala-harris-record-on-police-body-cameras-fits-into-the-2020-debate-on-criminal-justice.

26. Rezzo, Salvador. "Why did Kamala Harris withhold support for special investigations of police shooting?" *Washington Post.* n.d. www.washingtonpost.com/politics/2019/01/30/why-did-kamala-harris-withhold-support-special-investigations-police-shootings/?utm_term=.8bfe6f12b9c5.

27. Chokshi, Niraj. "California could become the first state to ban the 'gay panic' defense." *Washington Post.* Last modified September 5, 2014. www.washingtonpost.com/blogs/govbeat/wp/2014/09/05/california-could-become-the-first-state-to-ban-the-gay-panic-defense/?utm_term=.f1c2e00aed89 percent20.

28. "Assembly Bill No. 2501: An act to amend Section 192 of the Penal Code, relating to man-slaughter." California Legislative Information. Accessed April 20, 2019. leginfo.legislature.ca .gov/faces/billTextClient.xhtml?bill_id=201320140AB2501.

29. Chappell, Carmen. "Kamala Harris' Complicated History with Wall Street Will Come Under Scrutiny in the 2020 Race." CNBC. Last modified January 23, 2019. www.cnbc.com/2019/01 /26/kamala-harris-has-complicated-history-with-wall-street.html.

30. California Monitor. "By the Numbers: Mortgage Relief across California." Last modified September 24, 2013. oag.ca.gov/sites/all/files/agweb/pdfs/mortgage_settlement/04-report-by-the -numbers.pdf.

31. "Kamala D. Harris Oped: California Needs a Homeowner Bill of Rights." *Los Angeles Daily News.* Last modified August 28, 2017. www.dailynews.com/2012/04/16/kamala-d-harris-oped -california-needs-a-homeowner-bill-of-rights/.

32. Gordon, Amy Lofts. "California Foreclosure Protection: The Homeowner Bill of Rights." *Nolo .com.* Last modified December 12, 2012. www.nolo.com/legal-encyclopedia/california-foreclosure -protection-the-new-homeowner-bill-rights.html.

33. Harris, Kamala D. "Attorney General Kamala D. Harris Announces the California Homeowner Bill of Rights to Take Effect on January 1." Last modified July 28, 2016. oag.ca.gov/news/press -releases/attorney-general-kamala-d-harris-announces-california-homeowner-bill-rights-take.

34. Graham, Darwin Bond. "The Strike Force That Never Struck." *East Bay Express.* Last modified May 28, 2014. www.eastbayexpress.com/oakland/the-strike-force-that-never-struck/Content?oid =3933743.

35. Dayen, David. "Treasury Nominee Steve Mnuchin's Bank Accused of 'Widespread Misconduct' In Leaked Memo." *The Intercept.* Last modified January 3, 2017. theintercept.com/2017/01/03 /treasury-nominee-steve-mnuchins-bank-accused-of-widespread-misconduct-in-leaked-memo/.

36. Lane, Sylvan. "Dem Defends Decision Not to Charge Trump Treasury Pick over Foreclosures." *The Hill.* Last modified January 5, 2017. thehill.com/policy/finance/312742-senate-democrat -defends-decision-not-to-charge-trump-treasury-pick-over.

37. "Kamala Harris' Bureau of Children's Justice Takes Shape." *Chronicle of Social Change.* Last modified January 25, 2019. chronicleofsocialchange.org/multimedia/kamala-harris-bureau-of -childrens-justice-taking-shape/9513.

38. Harris, Kamala. Facebook. Last modified June 7, 2015. www.facebook.com/KamalaHarris/posts /when-i-created-the-bureau-of-childrens-justice-i-did-it-for-one-reason-we-cant-l/ 10153746509957923/.

39. "Bureau of Children's Justice." Last modified May 18, 2018. oag.ca.gov/bcj.

40. Loudenback, Jeremy. "California Bureau of Children's Justice Launches Five Investigations." *Chronicle of Social Change.* Last modified June 28, 2016. chronicleofsocialchange.org/child -welfare-2/calif-bureau-childrens-justice-launches-five-investigations.

41. Stanberry, Linda. "Agreement Reached in Attorney General's HumCo Child Abuse Reporting Inquiry." *North Coast Journal.* Last modified February 15, 2018. www.northcoastjournal.com /NewsBlog/archives/2018/02/15/settlement-reached-in-attorney-generals-humco-child-abuse -reporting-inquiry.

42. Males, Mike. "California Decision Aims to End Aggressive Policing in Schools." *YES! Magazine.* Last modified February 14, 2019. www.yesmagazine.org/people-power/california-decision-aims -to-end-aggressive-policing-in-schools-20190214.

43. Ibid.

44. Habte, Samson. "Prosecutor May Keep License After Doctoring Evidence." Bloomberg BNA. Last modified December 14, 2016. www.bna.com/prosecutor-may-keep-n73014448580/.

45. Bazelon, Emily. "Kamala Harris, a 'Top Cop' in the Era of Black Lives Matter." *New York Times.* Last modified January 19, 2018. www.nytimes.com/2016/05/29/magazine/kamala-harris-a-top-cop-in-the-era-of-black-lives-matter.html.

46. Ibid.

47. Habte, Samson. "Prosecutor May Keep License After Doctoring Evidence." Bloomberg BNA. Last modified December 14, 2016. www.bna.com/prosecutor-may-keep-n73014448580/.

48. Bazelon, Emily. "Kamala Harris, a 'Top Cop?' in the Era of Black Lives Matter." *New York Times.* Last modified January 19, 2018. www.nytimes.com/2016/05/29/magazine/kamala-harris-a-top-cop-in-the-era-of-black-lives-matter.html.

49. Moxley, Scott. "California Justices Hand DA Tony Rackauckas His Latest Embarrassment." *OC Weekly.* Last modified February 15, 2019. ocweekly.com/california-justices-hand-da-tony-rackauckas-his-latest-embarrassment-7695337/.

50. Newberry, Laura. "Orange County Voters Appear to Oust Longtime Dist. Atty. Tony Rackauckas." *Los Angeles Times.* Last modified November 7, 2018. www.latimes.com/local/lanow/la-me-ln-orange-county-district-attorney-race-20181106-story.html.

51. Ibid.

52. Cohen, Andrew. "The Accuser's Mom Called Her a 'Pathological Liar' Nobody Told the Defense." Marshall Project. Last modified August 29, 2016. www.themarshallproject.org/2016/08/29/the-accuser-s-mom-called-her-a-pathological-liar-nobody-told-the-defense.

53. Maura Dolan. "State to Double Crime Searches Using Family DNA." *Los Angeles Times.* Last modified March 14, 2019. www.latimes.com/local/la-xpm-2011-may-09-la-me-familial-dna-20110509-story.html.

54. Zhao, Christina. "How Was the Golden State Killer Caught? DNA from Relative on Genealogy Website Was Key." *Newsweek.* Last modified April 5, 2018. www.newsweek.com/how-was-golden-state-killer-caught-dna-relative-genealogy-website-was-key-903590.

55. Harris, Kamala D. "Attorney General Kamala D. Harris Announces Criminal Charges Against Senior Corporate Officers of Backpage.com for Profiting from Prostitution and Arrest of Carl Ferrer, CEO." Last modified October 6, 2016. oag.ca.gov/news/press-releases/attorney-general-kamala-d-harris-announces-criminal-charges-against-senior.

56. Jackman, Tom. "Backpage CEO Carl Ferrer pleads guilty in three states, agrees to testify against other website officials." *Washington Post.* Accessed April 20, 2019. www.washingtonpost.com/news/true-crime/wp/2018/04/13/backpage-ceo-carl-ferrer-pleads-guilty-in-three-states-agrees-to-testify-against-other-website-officials/?utm_term=.aff79984ba53.

57. Shaw, Donald. "How Kamala Harris Helped Her Hollywood Donors Censor the Web." *Sludge.* Last modified April 15, 2019. readsludge.com/2019/04/15/how-kamala-harris-helped-her-hollywood-donors-censor-the-web/.

58. Harris, Kamala D. "Protecting Health Care for All." *HuffPost.* Last modified May 5, 2015. www.huffpost.com/entry/king-v-burwell_b_6811494.

59. Smith, Doug, and Brittney Mejia. "Pipeline Company Indicted in 2015 Santa Barbara County Oil Spill." *Los Angeles Times.* Last modified May 18, 2016. www.latimes.com/local/lanow/la-me-ln-santa-barbara-county-oil-spill-20160517-snap-story.html.

60. Mcswain, Dan. "Will California Catch Oil Industry Price-Fixing?" *San Diego Union-Tribune*. Last modified July 6, 2016. www.sandiegouniontribune.com/business/sdut-california-investigates-oil-industry-price-fixing-2016jul06-story.html.

61. "Luis Alejo, Kamala Harris Back Asset Seizure before Criminal Charges." *Monterey Herald*. Last modified September 11, 2018. www.montereyherald.com/2015/02/23/luis-alejo-kamala-harris-back-asset-seizure-before-criminal-charges/.

62. Ollstein, Alice M. "California Attorney General Says Her Office's Defense of Prison Labor 'Evokes Chain Gangs?" *ThinkProgress*. Last modified November 19, 2014. thinkprogress.org/california-attorney-general-says-her-offices-defense-of-prison-labor-evokes-chain-gangs-5c768fd447a4/.

63. Lewis, Amanda. "The Prisoners Fighting California's Wildfires." *BuzzFeed*. Last modified October 31, 2014. www.buzzfeed.com/amandachicagolewis/the-prisoners-fighting-californias-wildfires.

64. Harris, Kamala D. "The Arizona Immigration Law: Politics over Policy." *HuffPost*. Last modified December 6, 2017. www.huffpost.com/entry/the-arizona-immigration-l_b_568209.

65. Roth, Tanya. "AG Kamala Harris Submits Brief in Support of Sergio Garcia." Findlaw. Last modified July 24, 201. blogs.findlaw.com/california_case_law/2012/07/ag-kamala-harris-submits-brief-in-support-of-sergio-garcia.html.

66. "California Attorney Who Fought to Practice Law Finally Gets Green Card." *The Guardian*. Last modified October 5, 2017. www.theguardian.com/us-news/2015/jun/04/california-attorney-green-card.

67. Camia, Catalina. "Calif. AG Kamala Harris Begins Senate Campaign." *USA Today*. Last modified January 13, 2015. www.usatoday.com/story/news/politics/elections/2015/01/13/kamala-harris-california-senate-boxer/21685953/.

68. "2016 United States Senate Election in California." Wikipedia. Last modified September 9, 2014. en.wikipedia.org/wiki/2016_United_States_Senate_election_in_California.

69. Seitz-Wald, Alex. "Elizabeth Warren Goes All In for Kamala Harris." MSNBC. Last modified January 14, 2015. www.msnbc.com/msnbc/elizabeth-warren-goes-all-kamala-harris#55681.

70. Garofoli, Joe. "Jerry Brown's Endorsement of Kamala Harris May Win Independents." *SFGate*. Accessed April 20, 2019. www.sfgate.com/politics/article/Jerry-Brown-s-endorsement-of-Kamala-Harris-may-7940531.php.

71. Roarty Alex, National Journal. "Posh Hotels and Pricey Airfare: Meet the Senate Candidate Driving Democrats Crazy." *The Atlantic*. Last modified December 6, 2015. www.theatlantic.com/politics/archive/2015/12/posh-hotels-and-pricey-airfare-meet-the-senate-candidate-driving-democrats-crazy/436620/.

72. Williams, Vanessa, and Catherine Ho. "Kamala Harris handily wins California Senate primary, Sanchez running second." *Washington Post*. Last modified June 8, 2016. www.washingtonpost.com/politics/kamala-harris-wins-california-senate-primary-rep-sanchez-in-second-place/2016/06/08/b0c2a2f0-2c08-11e6-b5db-e9bc84a2c8e4_story.html?utm_term=.8acb20e1edd8.

73. Willon, Phil. "For Kamala Harris' Senate Campaign, the State Democratic Party's Endorsement Has Been a Jackpot." *Los Angeles Times*. Last modified September 29, 2016. www.latimes.com/politics/essential/la-pol-sac-essential-politics-updates-for-kamala-harris-the-endorsement-from-1475185967-htmlstory.html.

74. Williams, Vanessa, and Catherine Ho, op. cit.

75. Willon, Phil. "Obama, Biden Endorse Kamala Harris for U.S. Senate." *Baltimore Sun*. Last modified November 3, 2017. www.baltimoresun.com/la-pol-sac-essential-politics-updates -obama-biden-endorse-kamala-harris-for-1468889660-htmlstory.html.

76. Williams, Vanessa. "Loretta Sanchez blasts Obama for endorsing Kamala Harris in CA Senate race." *Washington Post*. Last modified July 19, 2016. www.washingtonpost.com/news/powerpost /wp/2016/07/19/obama-biden-endorse-kamala-harris-in-california-senate-race/?utm_term =.73905de4f67c.

77. Willon, Phil. "Supreme Court Speculation about Kamala Harris Shadows Senate Bid." *Los Angeles Times*. Last modified February 16, 2016. www.latimes.com/politics/la-pol-ca-kamala -harris-supreme-court-20160216-story.html.

78. Deena Zaru. "Loretta Sanchez Dabs in California Senate Debate, Kamala Harris Not Amused." CNN. Last modified October 6, 2016. www.cnn.com/2016/10/06/politics/california-senate-race -debate-dab-loretta-sanchez-kamala-harris/index.html.

79. "United States Senate Election in California, 2016." Ballotpedia. Accessed April 20, 2019. ballotpedia.org/United_States_Senate_election_in_California,_2016.

80. "Kamala Harris Speaks on Election Night." YouTube. November 9, 2016. Accessed April 20, 2019. www.youtube.com/watch?v=3K5leD-ZxOo&t=0s.

SENATE CAREER

1. "Kamala Harris Sworn in by VP Biden." C-SPAN.org. Last modified January 3, 2017. www.c-span .org/video/?c4640845/kamala-harris-sworn-vp-biden.

2. Brawley, Lucia. "Kamala Harris and Cory Booker Just Made Senate History." *Washington Press*. Last modified January 9, 2018. washingtonpress.com/2018/01/09/kamala-harris-cory-booker -just-made-senate-history/.

3. "A Resolution Condemning Hate Crime and Any Other Form of Racism, Religious or Ethnic Bias, Discrimination, Incitement to Violence, or Animus Targeting a Minority in the United States. (2017 - S.Res. 118)." GovTrack.us. Accessed April 22, 2019. www.govtrack.us/congress /bills/115/sres118.

4. "COUNT Victims Act (2018 - S. 3033)." GovTrack.us. Accessed April 22, 2019. www.govtrack .us/congress/bills/115/s3033.

5. Fink, Sheri. "Puerto Rico's Hurricane Maria Death Toll Could Exceed 4,000, New Study Estimates." *New York Times*. Last modified May 30, 2018. www.nytimes.com/2018/05/29/us /puerto-rico-deaths-hurricane.html?module=inline.

6. Santiago, Leyla, Catherine E. Shoichet, and Jason Kravarik. "Puerto Rico's New Hurricane Maria Death Toll is 46 Times higher Than the Government's Previous Count." CNN. Last modified August 28, 2018. www.cnn.com/2018/08/28/health/puerto-rico-gw-report-excess -deaths/index.html.

7. "Disaster Victims Passport and ID Relief Act of 2018 (2018 - S. 3055)." GovTrack.us. Accessed April 22, 2019. www.govtrack.us/congress/bills/115/s3055.

8. S.3178—115th Congress (2017-2018).

9. "Justice for Victims of Lynching Act of 2019 (S. 488)." GovTrack.us. Accessed April 22, 2019. www.govtrack.us/congress/bills/116/s488.

10. S.1593—115th Congress (2017-2018).

11. "John Muir National Historic Site Expansion Act (2017 - S. 729)." GovTrack.us. Accessed April 22, 2019. www.govtrack.us/congress/bills/115/s729.

12. "Saint Francis Dam Disaster National Memorial Act (S. 129)." GovTrack.us. Accessed April 22, 2019. www.govtrack.us/congress/bills/116/s129.

13. "Exchange between Sen. Harris and CIA Director Nominee on Torture (C-SPAN)." YouTube. May 9, 2018. www.youtube.com/watch?v=nBR95rbQR7c.

14. Garofoli, Joe. "Kamala Harris Says She'll Vote against Gina Haspel as CIA Chief." *San Francisco Chronicle*. Last modified May 9, 2018. www.sfchronicle.com/politics/article/Kamala-Harris-says -she-ll-vote-against-Gina-12902239.php.

15. Harris, Kamala. "Harris Presses Facebook COO on Company's Revenue from Russian Propaganda, Hate Speech." Last modified September 5, 2018. www.harris.senate.gov/news/press-releases /harris-presses-facebook-coo-on-companys-revenue-from-russian-propaganda-hate-speech.

16. Ibid.

17. Homeland Security and Government Affairs. Pronounced "his-gack."

18. Harris, Kamala. Twitter. Accessed April 24, 2019. twitter.com/kamalaharris/status /1008784431694241792?lang=en.

19. Foran Clare. "Harris Calls for DHS Secretary to Resign." CNN. Last modified June 18, 2018. www.cnn.com/2018/06/18/politics/immigration-family-separation-kamala-harris-dhs-secretary /index.html.

20. "Sign the Petition: Kirstjen Nielsen Must Resign." Kamala Harris. Accessed April 24, 2019. action.kamalaharris.org/sign/petition-180618-nielsen/.

21. "Kamala Harris Receives an Orwellian Response from Kirstjen Nielsen." C-SPAN.org. Accessed April 24, 2019. www.c-span.org/video/?c4754678/kamala-harris-receives-orwellian-response -kirstjen-nielsen.

22. Ainsley, Julia. "Trump Admin Weighed Denying Asylum Hearings for Separated Migrant Kids." *NBC News*. Last modified January 18, 2019. www.nbcnews.com/politics/immigration /trump-admin-weighed-targeting-migrant-families-speeding-deportation-children-n958811.

23. Merkley, Senator Jeff. "Merkley Reveals Secret Trump Administration Plan to Create Border Crisis." *Medium*. Last modified January 18, 2019. medium.com/@SenJeffMerkley/merkley -reveals-secret-trump-administration-plan-to-create-border-crisis-f72a7c3de2bd.

24. "Kamala Harris's 2018 Legislative Statistics." GovTrack.us. Accessed April 22, 2019. www .govtrack.us/congress/members/kamala_harris/412678/report-card/2018.

25. Stein, Jeff. "Kamala Harris's Immigration Gamble." *Vox*. Last modified November 1, 2017. www.vox.com/policy-and-politics/2017/11/1/16554958/kamala-harris-immigration-california.

26. Wire, Sarah D. "Sen. Kamala Harris Pushes to Guarantee Access to Legal Counsel for Those Detained Upon Entry to the U.S." *Los Angeles Times*. Last modified February 9, 2017. www .latimes.com/politics/essential/la-pol-ca-essential-politics-updates-sen-kamala-harris-pushes-for -right-to-1486678257-htmlstory.html.

27. "Harris Statement on Immigration Vote." Last modified February 15, 2018. www.harris.senate .gov/news/press-releases/harris-statement-on-immigration-vote.

28. Manchester, Julia. "Harris: Trump Should Resign over Sexual Misconduct Allegations." *The Hill*. Last modified December 14, 2017. thehill.com/homenews/senate/364941-harris-trump-should -resign-over-sexual-misconduct-allegations-in-the-best.

29. Siders, David. Twitter. Accessed April 24, 2019. twitter.com/davidsiders/status /941369211145814016.

30. "Fox News Was Just Forced to Issue a Humiliating Apology over Insulting Kamala Harris Segment." *Washington Press.* Last modified October 23, 2018. washingtonpress.com/2018/10/23/fox-news-was-just-forced-to-issue-a-humiliating-apology-over-insulting-kamala-harris-segment/.

31. Koseff, Alexei. "Kamala Harris Aide Resigns After Harassment, Retaliation Settlement Surfaces." *Sacramento Bee.* Last modified December 5, 2018. www.sacbee.com/news/politics-government/capitol-alert/article222688740.html.

32. Summers, Juana, Alan Suderman, and Stephen Braun. "Kamala Harris Is Latest 2020 Dem Contender to Release Taxes." AP News. Last modified April 14, 2019. www.apnews.com/7f506fc56d4b48ba8699bb3dccc75606.

ANALYSIS: HARRIS'S CHANCES FOR WINNING THE NOMINATION AND PRESIDENCY

1. Solei, Stacey. "Kamala Harris Kicks Off 2020 Campaign with Oakland Rally." *New York Times.* Last modified January 28, 2019. www.nytimes.com/2019/01/27/us/politics/kamala-harris-rally-2020.html.

2. "Election 2020 - 2020 Democratic Presidential Nomination." *RealClearPolitics.* Accessed April 24, 2019. www.realclearpolitics.com/epolls/2020/president/us/2020_democratic_presidential_nomination-6730.html#polls.

3. Karanth, Sanjana. "Kamala Harris Says Her Presidential Campaign Has Raised $12 Million." *HuffPost.* Last modified April 1, 2019. www.huffpost.com/entry/kamala-harris-12-million-presidential-campaign_n_5ca2cd83e4b04693a9465026.

4. "Candidate for president contributions: Kamala Harris." Federal Election Commission. Accessed April 24, 2019. www.fec.gov/data/candidate/P00009423/.

5. Ibid.

6. Kamala, Harris. "Kamala Comments about her campaign." Twitter. Accessed April 24, 2019. twitter.com/KamalaHarris/status/1112879795501764610.

7. "Evaluating the 2020 Democratic Primary Field." *RealClearPolitics.* Last modified April 9, 2019. www.realclearpolitics.com/articles/2019/04/09/evaluating_the_2020_democratic_primary_field_139997.html.

8. Alonso-Zaldivar, Ricardo. "Poll: Support for 'Medicare-for-All' Fluctuates with Details." AP News. Last modified January 23, 2019. www.apnews.com/4516833e7fb644c9aa8bcc11048b2169.

9. Phone interview by author.

10. Harris, Kamala. "Our America." Accessed April 24, 2019. kamalaharris.org/our-america/.

11. "Election 2020 - 2020 Democratic Presidential Nomination." *RealClearPolitics.* Accessed April 24, 2019. www.realclearpolitics.com/epolls/2020/president/us/2020_democratic_presidential_nomination-6730.html#polls.

12. Sparks, Grace. "New Poll: Buttigieg Surges into Top Tier in New Hampshire." CNN. Last modified April 23, 2019. www.cnn.com/2019/04/22/politics/unh-poll-march-buttigieg-biden-sanders/index.html.

13. Cadelago, Christopher. "New Hampshire Gives Harris a Hard Time for Rarely Showing Up." *Politico.* Last modified February 19, 2019. www.Politico.com/story/2019/02/19/new-hampshire-kamala-harris-1173820.

14. Hughes, Greg, and John King. "Elizabeth Warren's Polling Problem: Gaining Support from Next Door." CNN. Last modified March 4, 2019. www.cnn.com/2019/03/03/politics/inside-politics-forecast-march-3-cnntv/index.html?no-st=1553567090.

15. "Election 2020 - Iowa Democratic Presidential Caucus." *RealClearPolitics*. Accessed April 24, 2019. www.realclearpolitics.com/epolls/2020/president/ia/iowa_democratic_presidential _caucus-6731.html.

16. "South Carolina 2020 Poll: Biden Leads Primary Field by Wide Margin; President Trump Popular with Base." Emerson Polling Reportable News. Accessed April 24, 2019. emersonpolling .reportablenews.com/pr/south-carolina-2020-poll-biden-leads-primary-field-by-wide-margin -president-trump-popular-with-base.

17. Ashain, Andy S. "Biden still leads but Abrams, Buttigieg join front-runners in new SC 2020 primary poll." *Post and Courier*. Last modified April 8, 2019. www.postandcourier.com/politics /biden-still-leads-but-abrams-buttigieg-join-front-runners-in/article_2c8f9d32-57eb-11e9-abc5 -531783c41f18.html.

18. Rodrigo, Chris M. "Sanders Leads Poll of Young Democrats by Double Digits." *The Hill*. Last modified April 1, 2019. thehill.com/homenews/campaign/436675-sanders-leads-poll-of-young -democratic-voters-by-double-digits.

19. "Wisconsin 2020: Bernie Sanders Leads Democratic Field; Trump Competitive in General Election." Emerson Polling Reportable News. Accessed April 24, 2019. emersonpolling .reportablenews.com/pr/ wisconsin-2020-bernie-sanders-leads-democratic-field-trump-competitive-in-general-election.

20. Marinucci, Carla. "Harris Unveils California Endorsements in Home State Show of Force." *Politico*. Last modified February 7, 2019. www.Politico.com/story/2019/02/07/kamala-harris-2020 -california-endorsments-1157651.

21. Ibid.

22. Cadelago, Christopher. "Gavin Newsom Endorses Kamala Harris for President." *Politico*. Last modified February 15, 2019. www.Politico.com/story/2019/02/15/gavin-newsom-endorses-kamala -harris-2020-1173317.

23. Kinnard, Meg. "Kamala Harris Picks Up New Endorsements in Early-Voting South Carolina." *Post and Courier*. Last modified April 23, 2019. www.postandcourier.com/politics/state_politics /kamala-harris-picks-up-new-endorsements-in-early-voting-south/article_3b3012c2-55c3-51d9 -9820-3fd026ad3ebb.html.

24. Kinnard, Meg. "Kamala Harris Lands Diverse Endorsements in South Carolina." AP News. Last modified March 28, 2019. apnews.com/dcbd01bb674e468b85b5b11b5509ba69.

25. Harris, Kamala. *Making It Plain*. Interview by Mark Thompson. SiriusXM, April 5, 2019.

26. "Kamala Harris Presidential Campaign, 2020." Ballotpedia. Accessed April 24, 2019. ballotpedia .org/Kamala_Harris_presidential_campaign,_2020.

27. "Election 2020 - General Election: Trump vs. Harris." *RealClearPolitics*. Accessed April 24, 2019. www.realclearpolitics.com/epolls/2020/president/us/general_election_trump_vs_harris -6252.html.

28. Allen, Jonathan. "Why the 2020 Democratic Primary Could Turn into 'Lord of the Flies.'" *NBC News*. Last modified January 24, 2019. www.nbcnews.com/politics/2020-election/why-2020 -democratic-primary-could-turn-lord-flies-n961236.